Your Heart and Money:
Uncover the Lies and Live Free

The
Stewardship Movement

Katelyn A. Swiatek

The Stewardship Movement
Published by Tek Inc. (dba MAP Financial Solutions)
4164 Austin Bluffs Pkwy, #122
Colorado Springs, CO 80918

www.MapFinancialSolutions.com

All Scripture quotations, unless otherwise indicated, are taken from the Holy Bible, New International Version®. Copyright © 1973, 1978, 1984 by International Bible Society. Used by permission of Zondervan. All rights reserved.

Scripture quotations marked (MSG) are taken from the Message, by Eugene H. Peterson. Copyright © 1993, 1994, 1995, 1996, 2000, 2001, 2002. Used by permission of NavPress Publishing Group.

Scripture quotations marked (KJV) are taken from the King James Version.

Italics or parentheses in Scripture quotations reflect the author's added emphasis.

ISBN 978-0-9860910-0-1
ISBN 978-0-9860910-1-8 (electronic)

Copyright © 2015 by Katelyn A. Swiatek

Cover image and author photo by Taryn Ryan Long. Cover design and images Copyright © 2015 Tek Inc.

All rights reserved. No part of this book may be reproduced or transmitted in any form or by any means, electronic or mechanical, including photocopying and recording, or by any information storage or retrieval system, without permission in writing from the publisher.

Published in the United States by Tek Inc. (dba MAP Financial Solutions).

MAP Financial Solutions is a registered trademark of Tek Inc.

Library of Congress Cataloging-in-Publication Data is on file at the Library of Congress, Washington, DC.

Printed in the United States of America

Sales and Author Contact
This book is available at a discount if purchased in bulk. The author is available for training and guest visits. For more information, please email MAP Financial Solutions at info@mapfinancialsolutions.com.

This book is dedicated to those suffering each day to make ends meet by rummaging through the garbage dumps. May God's grace shine upon you and may you hear the hope of His love.

"He raiseth up the poor out of the dust,
and lifteth the needy out of the dunghill."
Psalm 113:7, KJV

Thirty percent of the net profit on each book will be donated toward ministries that work to bring individuals living in trash dumps worldwide dignity, nutrition, education, and the hope of the gospel.

I also want to express my gratitude for my husband, Stephen. Thank you for believing in me and supporting my calling. Thank you for giving me the push I needed when I was unsure of myself, and thank you for being so proud of me! I love you.

Thank you to Teri, for standing by my side through this process and pouring your time and soul into this book with me. Thank you for the countless hours you have spent editing and helping me to solidify this message.

And thank you to all of the clients and students whom I've had the privilege to serve. Thank you for teaching me all that you did in our time together. It was an honor to work with you. You have left an eternal impression on my heart.

Contents

Part I: Learn

Introduction — 9

Chapter 1: The Giving Cycle — 14

Chapter 2: Uncovering the Root — 24

Chapter 3: Understanding Poverty — 28

Chapter 4: Understanding Wealth — 39

Chapter 5: The Lack of Nobility in Poverty — 58

Chapter 6: Handling Wealth Generously — 71

Chapter 7: What Is Tithing Today — 80

Part II: Live

Chapter 8: Financial Management — 94

Chapter 9: Setting Goals and Budgeting — 101

Chapter 10: Tackling Debt — 125

Chapter 11: Creating Savings — 139

Conclusion — 155

Part I: Learn

Introduction

In February of 2013, I found myself running out of a hotel in Dallas, Texas. Before I tell you how I got there, let me start here:

Over the last few years, I have developed an aversion to flying. As a child, I would fly all over the country, but lately flying anywhere terrifies me, Dallas included. The turbulence in Dallas tops my most dreaded destinations list. The last flight I took into Dallas had me praying out loud on the landing, raising several eyebrows! The pilot didn't stick the landing on the first try, and before I knew it, we were at the end of the runway. Then our nose shot up. We went from ten feet off the ground to what felt like ten thousand in thirty seconds. We did land safely in the end—thank you, Lord, for the power of prayer! However, let's just say my relationship with the Dallas airport does not hold a warm place in my heart. And as for that hotel, its days were numbered. I ended up at another place across the interstate and kissed the floor upon arrival!

However, there is one event for which I will brave the airplane turbulence and hotel trauma of Dallas, and that's the Christian Stewardship Network Forum. I attended this forum in February 2013 after finding out about it from a church-stewardship director named Dave. I met Dave for the first time when he came to our church, offering a stewardship seminar to local church planters. I was like a kid in a candy store as I heard him talk about biblical financial stewardship. He was one of my kind! Within a few weeks, I was in Dallas. And it was on this trip that God clarified His vision and calling for my life.

I didn't start out a *math whiz*, and I am still not one. In school, my strongest subjects were English, history and art—anything but math!

I remember having a private tutor help me with my multiplication because I was just not getting it. Looking back, I simply didn't care. It was not that I was less gifted. I just didn't invest my time into something I thought was boring.

My turning point with numbers came in 2009 when I assumed the role of a general manager for a 124-unit apartment community. In this position I had to analyze the financials and report to the owner on the bottom line. I was forced to understand numbers. Soon after this, about a year after Stephen and I were married, I realized that in marriage, I could not fake it anymore. I was terrible with numbers. It became clear to me that in order to manage a budget with my husband, I had to *get* numbers. So we created our first budget using Microsoft Excel and attempted to live by it. It was a disaster. I would continually blow off the budget. While I felt good that we had a budget, I didn't utilize it as a boundary line for our spending—budget smudget!

In my work world, after my role as a general manager, I transitioned to working directly for the CFO of a Christian digital company, reporting financials to the CFO, CEO, board, and authors. This company was brand new, so once again I was dropped into the fire. Let's just say that after this, our family budget got fine-tuned, and I started to pay serious attention to the numbers. Unfortunately this company dissolved, and the CEO referred me to be an assistant to one of the board members. He was a successful life-insurance agent, and I learned a tremendous amount about the life-insurance industry working for him. This is when God started to prick my heart about finances. I realized that whether you think you're good at math or not, it doesn't matter to God. We're all called to manage our finances wisely, and there is no excuse for poor management. Soon after this, I became a licensed life-insurance producer in Colorado and Nevada. In the process of assisting my clients, God opened my eyes to an even deeper need than life insurance—*financial management training*. While my clients were taking care of their life insurance, their spending habits could eventually cost them heavily in the end. God started to lead me down the path toward financial counseling. God revealed to me a system that works for people, a system that frees people from the rice and bean approach and gives them leeway to enjoy life, save money, and pay down debt—all at the same time!

That was the beginning of *The Stewardship Movement*. I have been blessed with success stories from all over, and I am honored to have served couples, individuals, and businesses. I am humbled that these clients trusted me enough to let me into one of the most private areas of their lives and mentor them toward their goals.

All this brings us back to the 2013 CSN forum in Dallas. I was counseling couples and individuals, but I still felt like God was tugging on my heart for more. At the forum, I felt the Lord shift my focus from individuals to church leadership. He called me to immerse myself in the study of biblical financial stewardship. I felt Him say to me that if I wanted to make the impact that my heart desired (igniting a passion for biblical stewardship in the lives of millions), I needed to start with church leaders. I especially saw this within my own church. They were gracious enough to allow me to teach the stewardship course I developed for individuals as a fall and spring study. The turnout was very cyclical, and I prayed fervently to God about why this was happening. It broke my heart that people didn't seem interested in such an important topic. I thought the turnout was related to how I was marketing the course, so I started to think of more creative ways to promote it. Yet as I continued to pray about it, God did not lead me to better marketing strategies. He led me to reach the leadership. He revealed that in order to ignite a passion for biblical stewardship in the lives of millions, the leaders had to get involved, especially the head pastor.

Think about it. How often do you think about money? If you said every day, bingo! Should you eat out for lunch today? How much is it to fill up your tank? Is your mortgage bill due soon? The list goes on and on. **Money is in our face every day, yet we often don't bring this topic through our church doors.** In many churches, money is talked about at the beginning of the new year, during a campaign for a new program, and maybe in a few other sermons. I can understand why pastors don't talk about money: it tends to turn people off, and they definitely don't want to hear about it at church. On top of this, many pastors fear offending members or coming across too pushy. While I understand all of these reasons, I encourage your church to take a stand: decide today that you want to help your church, your leadership, and your members have a *better* relationship with money. Money is something that we *all* deal with every day, rich or poor. Why not turn this relationship into one that is positive and grounded? **Until we can release whatever baggage we have in our lives in regard to money (or anything else), we will never be free.** Those who are generous are free. We need a movement of generosity within the Christian community, as it is a testament of our faith and brings glory to the Father (2 Cor. 9:6–15). You have the opportunity to turn around the lives of those you shepherd so that they might be used to sow generously into Kingdom work. This is what is being missed. **It isn't about tithing to your church: it is about sowing generously into the Kingdom. But until the negative relationship with money is broken, this generosity cannot be released!** Think of all the opportunities being missed as you are reading this. In order to start addressing this in your church, you must determine if you can agree with these three statements. If so, you are ready:

1. I want church leadership and the members to have a better relationship with money. I want them to know what it means to sow generously into the Kingdom of God.

2. I accept that this process isn't about hype or manipulation to grow my church. I want our church to be instrumental in living out our mission, thus advancing the Kingdom of God and creating eternal impact.

3. I am ready to start with my personal finances. I understand that as a good leader, I must live out what I am teaching those around me to do.

This is just the beginning, and *The Stewardship Movement* will help your church get there. This movement is about igniting a passion for biblical financial stewardship in your church and beyond. This passion will enable you to empower your leadership and members to be free! In turn, those impacted can encourage others to do the same. This book isn't about what you are doing wrong as a church, nor is it just about budgeting and how to save more. ***The Stewardship Movement* is about equipping you with the truth of God's Word and what it has to say about money, so that in turn, you can raise up those you serve to live free!**

Chapter 1:
The Giving Cycle

There are many churches financially struggling today. Some feel the burden and pressure of debt. Others battle a constant lack of income. The majority are highly dependent upon their members' giving. While finances will never be guaranteed, there is a way to correct this struggle. First, your church's income cannot be the primary focus of your ministry. This can be very hard because of the dependence on income, but realigning your focus is critical. Take your focus off the income and direct it *toward* the people you serve.

Under the Mosaic Law, tithing 10 percent was a command. So people were obligated to give. Many people attending church today also feel obligated to give because they've been told it's what they're supposed to do. What if we could turn this thinking around? What if we can, through a better understanding of money from God's perspective, create a stir within our churches that ignites generosity? The goal of *The Stewardship Movement* is to help you do this. But before this can happen, we need to correct the broken giving cycle.

The Broken Giving Cycle

Your church is dependent on three things—God, people, and money. Sure, there are other factors that come together to make up a great church, but without these three things, you have no church. In order for your church to grow, let alone keep the lights on, you rely on your members to give. When the relationship between you and your members is broken, you are operating in a broken giving cycle.

The Broken Giving Cycle

Your church needs more funds, and perhaps you think that your members are the problem; they're not giving enough. So to address this issue, you preach a sermon on the importance of giving. This is in an effort to bring awareness to the issue. In response, your message creates a giving flurry. However, giving soon drops off, and you and your church leaders are left scratching your heads.

While some of your church members respond positively to the message, others are outraged. They become offended. So in an effort not to offend more, you pull back from preaching on giving. After all, you don't want to lose givers! Yet the givers that you fear losing aren't giving anyway.

Perhaps over time the Holy Spirit kneads your heart. You realize that if you want your members to give, then you and your leadership need to be living out financial stewardship in your own lives. You get excited and ride this momentous wave of revelation. Yet soon you become dismayed as the push fizzles out. Maybe giving and generosity aren't based on a formula? Maybe they originate from the heart?

Because you and your church leadership aren't living out what you are asking your members to live out, the message isn't sticking. Now your church is stuck, and not advancing the mission God has given you due to lack of funds—not only from your members, but also from your leadership. And so the cycle continues.

What Is the Broken Giving Cycle?

A broken giving cycle occurs when you become too focused on the bottom line rather than the people you serve and the mission that God has given you. Money will advance the calling and mission of your church, but in order to create a healthy giving cycle, you have to get some elements right. An occasional sermon on giving can be very effective, but not in the long run. Plus, teaching on financial stewardship can be very intimidating when you feel like you wrestle with what Scripture says about it. Yet it is very important that you address the finances in your church because **your church is dependent upon healthy finances for survival.**

I want to take a moment to encourage those of you feeling intimidated by this topic. As you read in the introduction, finances intimidated me for a majority of my life. They intimidated me until I realized that money is a relationship that I will have to steward the rest of my life. Plus, the way we manage money deeply affects our relationship with God. On top of this, if we are leaders, our decisions about money will affect those we serve, as well. While we can never hope to live up to every word we teach about finances, it is important that we cover it and that we don't avoid it because of our own shortcomings.

> Not many of you should presume to be teachers, my brothers, because you know that we who teach will be judged more strictly. We all stumble in many ways. If anyone is never at fault in what he says, he is a perfect man, able to keep his whole body in check.
> James 3:1–2

James 3:1–2 is clear in its warning, yet it extends us the grace we need to press forward. May we remember that Jesus was the Teacher: we are teachers. Jesus was Perfect: we are imperfect. Therefore, when it comes to your personal finances and those of your church, **it is not about getting it perfect.** It's about studying what God's Word has to say about finances and uncovering His truth so that you and your church can live free!

Live Free

> It is for freedom that Christ has set us free. Stand firm, then, and do not let yourselves be burdened again by a yoke of slavery.
> Galatians 5:1

If you constantly worry about your personal finances and those of your church, then you are enslaved. It is slavery to be caught up in anything that is not focused on God. Because money is such a large part of our lives and the lives of those we serve, it is critical that we grasp how to manage it in a way that glorifies God and advances His Kingdom. Biblical financial stewardship is not solely about budgeting, saving more, and avoiding debt. It's about catching God's vision for His Kingdom. In Christ, we have been set free from many things, but no one has ever been set free from having to think about money on a daily basis. Therefore, it's time to teach yourself how to have a healthy relationship with money and then teach your church members to do the same. The natural progression will be that you, your church leadership, and your members will become freer! It is very important to remember that the members of your church are directly influenced by what comes from you (the pulpit). If you are pumped about biblical financial stewardship and the passion for it resides in your heart, then talking about it in your sermons will be natural, not staged.

Money Is Necessary

We need money to advance the Kingdom of God. No, God does not need money, but we do, and so do our churches! In order to fulfill His mission through us and in the lives of those we serve, money is a critical component. If you don't believe this, then don't pay your bills for a month. When your electricity gets shut off, pray that God will turn the lights back on. Money turns the lights back on. In the long run, this pattern of thinking will not help anyone. It is not that God is not powerful enough, but we live on earth where it takes money for these things—there is no way around it.

In most churches, discussion on financial stewardship tends to be trigger based: we're building a new building...we're starting a new ministry...we're opening a café; therefore, we need more money. These triggers in turn spark a sermon or two on the importance of giving and the need for money in order to bring these projects to fruition. (I am not saying that all churches function this way.) From a business perspective, this sequence makes logical sense. Yet, in relation to how God operates, I am not quite sure it's enough. As noted in the broken giving cycle, you can get people riled up, but this kind of giving eventually drops off.

A few years back, Stephen and I went out to Utah for an author's seminar. It provided helpful teaching and we retained a lot of great information. We were pleased that the seminar was more about teaching than about selling the author's materials. During the seminar, we befriended one of the author's partners, and we were back a year later to attend his seminar—and what a difference between the two trainings! While the first was full of teaching, the second was a giant pitch fest. For about twenty minutes on the tail end of each teaching block, the audience was barraged with a bunch of hype in an effort to sell products at a one-time discount. By the end of the seminar, it became so predictable, and it was driving me crazy. What disgusted me the most was the manipulation of people. To me, it was a soft form of extortion. This company kept getting richer and richer off this method, tugging on people's emotions and empowering them falsely in order to get more money—horrible.

I hate to say this, but I feel like a lot of churches are falling into this trap with their fund-raising campaigns. While it may not be to the degree of that second seminar, we're still stirring up emotion among the masses to get them to give—and it works! But that doesn't make it right or honorable to God.

The Stewardship Movement is not about hype or manipulating people. It's about igniting a passion for biblical financial stewardship in the lives of millions to spur on the advancement of God's Kingdom.

This movement is about converting a broken giving cycle into one that breeds the advancement of the Kingdom. Generally, if a church is dependent on using hype campaigns, then they are caught in a broken giving cycle. This broken cycle seeks to lead and then grow, neglecting the rest of the important elements as shown in the diagram.

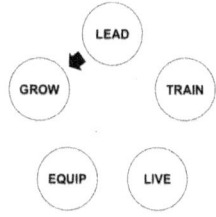

In order to correct this broken cycle, we need to add these critical components: training up ourselves and our staff on principles of biblical financial stewardship; collectively living out what we've learned; and then equipping our church members with materials that will teach them about biblical financial stewardship, which will enrich their lives. The cycle will then look like this:

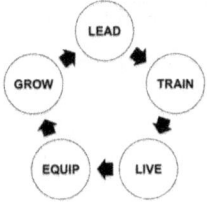

Implementing the Giving Cycle

First Step—Lead

You, the pastor of your church, need to commit to lead before anything else can move forward. Why you? You have an unspoken authority over your church. Members come because they trust you and your teaching. They have chosen to follow your instruction; you are their shepherd. In order to ignite a passion for biblical stewardship within your church, you must feel passionate about it. While you may not feel this passion yet, it is my hope that you will by the time you finish this book.

You will need to be the one who takes the initial lead to get your team excited about this topic. Then together, you can empower your church members, too.

The Stewardship Movement will arm you with the materials you need to do this, coupled with the journey that you will take in your heart.

Second Step—Train

Just like any good teacher, you must "train yourself up" before you can teach others. In order to ignite this passion in you and your leadership, you must first learn what God's Word has to say about finances and how to manage them His way. This will create a spark in your leadership that will be contagious to members. The only way to do this, as the leadership of your church, is collectively. Gather your team together for an hour per week for eight weeks. Use *The Stewardship Movement Video Series and Study Guide* for these study times. In this series, I do the teaching for you. You can access these videos and study guide at www.TheStewardshipMovement.com.

Third Step—Live

As you well know, when we first come to Christ, we rarely experience a complete and instant transformation. It takes time for His truths to soak into our hearts and for us to cultivate a relationship with Him. The same goes for this transformational journey. It will not be an instant change. You may even find your spirit resisting it. It takes time to get to a place where we're living something out. First, our hearts have to change. Then over time, this change becomes evident in our speech and actions (the fruit).

In order to start living this out, you have to start by choosing to live differently. This may be as simple as monitoring or cutting back on your spending. Others will see these changes, and your behavior can draw them closer to the truth about money while glorifying God in the process. That's what it's all about, right?

Fourth Step—Equip

Just as we feed our church body with the Word of God on various topics, it is time to feed them truths about money. There is a big difference when you serve them from the perspective of "we need you" versus "we want to set you free." This form of equipping is not rooted in an effort to amass money out of greed or need. It is about equipping those you serve to be free from the worry of money.

Fifth Step—Grow
Growth is inevitable when you start to apply God's principles about financial management to your life. It's the beauty of order that God put into the universe—cause and effect. The growth implied here is not an explosion of crops for hoarding but rather the necessary provision to advance the Kingdom of God through your church. A great depiction of this is illustrated in the parable of the sower. Work to create good soil within your church so that your members can in turn grow:

> "Those along the path are the ones who hear (*your church members*), and then the devil comes and takes away the word from their hearts, so that they may not believe and be saved. Those on the rock are the ones who receive the word with joy when they hear it, but they have no root. They believe it for a while, but in time of testing they fall away. The seed that fell among thorns stands for those who hear, but as they go on their way they are choked by life's worries, riches and pleasures, and they do not mature. But the seed on the good soil stands for those with a noble and good heart, who hear the word, retain it, and by persevering produce a crop."
> Luke 8:12–15 (Emphasis added.)

The Stewardship Movement is a resource for truths on biblical financial stewardship. In order to **lead** in this area, you will need to read and absorb this book in conjunction with Scripture. Do this as you are also working to **train up** your leadership team through *The Stewardship Movement Video Series and Study Guide*. This is critical, so they, too, can catch the vision. Together, you can **live out** principles of biblical financial stewardship in your own lives and **equip** your church members to do the same. Your church and the lives of those you serve **grow** in turn!

As the pastor, let reading the book and watching the video series be your first step toward leading. In the chapters that follow, we will tackle the following: where your money beliefs may have originated; what God has to say about poverty, wealth, and generosity; what giving looks like today under the New Covenant; and practical changes you can implement to gain confidence over your resources.

Together, let's ignite a Stewardship Movement in your church!

Chapter 2:
Uncovering the Root

Becoming a leader in the area of biblical financial stewardship starts with uncovering where your views about money originated. Just as we still do things a certain way because of how we grew up, we also view and manage money a certain way because of our backgrounds. The way we manage money stems from two things: first, our motives; second, our attitudes.

This part of the journey may expose some vulnerabilities, so can I suggest that we rip off the Band-Aid so that we can get on with it? If we don't, then we'll find ourselves ten steps ahead of where we need to be.

In order to lead others effectively, you must be willing to be vulnerable and face your muck. Money is an emotional topic, and many of us don't want to talk about it. I am still like this. Even today, when my husband brings up money, I feel my whole body lock up. I just don't like to talk about it. I don't even like to think about it. Yet as uncomfortable as these conversations are, we have to face money because if we don't, we're ignoring something that is very present in our lives.

Most of us grew up in a household where our parents (or those who raised us) had to handle money. How they dealt with it affected us, too. I knew a gentleman whose parents never saved, and they were always feeling stressed about never having savings. By his early thirties, he had over $100,000 saved up. He was terrified of being without. He also spent very conservatively in an effort to protect the money for which he worked. I could fill a whole book with examples like this, but what I want you to catch is the fact that your parents' thoughts and feelings rubbed off on you, big time! The goal of this chapter is to help you uncover how they rubbed off on you so that you can better understand where your attitudes about money originated. By understanding where your money attitudes originated, you will be able to face money today your own way, not necessarily the way your parents did.

To start getting your attitude right about money, quit telling yourself that you're not good with it, you will never have it, you always lose it, and so forth. By saying these things, you are placing curses over your finances (see Prov. 18:21). Even if you are not great with numbers, it does not mean that you can't train yourself to be. There is nowhere in Scripture where God says you don't have to worry about how to manage the affairs of your household. It actually says that you must, especially as an overseer, handle your affairs well.

> Here is a trustworthy saying: If anyone sets his heart on being an overseer, he desires a noble task. Now the overseer must be above reproach, the husband but of one wife, temperate, self-controlled, respectable, hospitable, able to teach, not given to drunkenness, not violent but gentle, not quarrelsome, not a lover of money. He must manage his own family well and see that his children obey him with proper respect. (If anyone does not know how to manage his own family, how can he take care of God's church?)
> 1 Timothy 3:1–5

Not only are we responsible for the matters of our home, but also we are responsible in God's church. Matters involving God's church include money and church's dependence on it. As the pastor of your church, you are probably not balancing the budget or preparing financial reports for your board, but it's still critical for you to understand what the numbers mean and what they say about the financial health of your church. When you understand the numbers for your household and church, you become an active participant. You are now choosing to take charge over these areas and are no longer functioning in fear.

Your Money Motives and Attitudes

Your attitudes about money affect your management of it. These attitudes can originate from your upbringing and also from motives. Part of uncovering the recesses of your heart includes examining your motives. And you thought the process was uncomfortable before?

For most of us, it can be a real struggle to sit in silence and seek our motives. But it can also be so rewarding and can lead to freedom.

At the end of this chapter, you will take the Money Quiz. This will not only help you identify where your money attitudes originated, but it will also help you uncover your motives. Motives originate from the heart, and the heart is what God is after. No matter how much you learn about biblical financial stewardship, if your heart is not right, then no growth will occur. We must bring our motives to the surface because money will always be in our lives. Our motives are revealed in our attitudes and management of money, in lean and in abundant times. Motives, good or bad, drive all behavior, and we are all subject to the occasional misdirection of them.

This reality is especially critical for leaders. A constant examination of motives is vital to ensure that your decisions are rooted in obedience and not in pride. In summary, money motives lead to money attitudes, and both of which are reflected in money management:

Money Motives → Money Attitudes → Money Management

In regard to the gentleman that I mentioned earlier, his motive was to never be poor. So his attitude was, "I will never be poor." Therefore, he managed his money in relation to his motive and attitude. By uncovering your motives and attitudes, you free yourself up to manage money more in line with God's truths. I want to encourage you that I still don't have this 100 percent right. I have managed our household budget and the finances of businesses, and I still don't have it perfect. So please know that it isn't about getting it perfect. It's about examining your heart in order to glorify the Father.

> But the Lord said to Samuel, "Do not consider his appearance or his height, for I have rejected him. The Lord does not look at the things man looks at. Man looks at the outward appearance, but the Lord looks at the heart."
> 1 Samuel 16:7

Now it's time for you to take the Money Quiz. Be sure to pray before taking it. There are going to be questions that you may feel are unimportant or too detailed. Give them your best effort. Over the years I have seen that the effort an individual puts into this quiz directly translates into the effort he or she is willing to put into his or her finances.

This quiz and the commitment to this process are the first and most critical steps. This quiz is designed to bring you awareness. There are no right answers; there is no score. It's just a mirror for you to see what's been going on in your heart (motives and attitudes). It's time to debunk the lies affecting your finances. Remember, if you don't start here, no matter how much you learn about this topic, you won't see change. You must start at the root—your heart. Take the Money Quiz now at www.TheStewardshipMovement.com.

Chapter 3:
Understanding Poverty

Now that you have brought your awareness to the surface through the Money Quiz, it is time to start learning more about what God's Word has to say about money. Money is a broad subject, and because of this, I have broken it down into three areas: poverty, wealth, and giving. The first is poverty.

When we talk about money, we know that there are people with a lot of it and also some with very little of it. So what does God say about poverty in Scripture? As we start to explore what He has to say, we can migrate toward His thinking and His heart in this area.

When you hear the words *poor* or *poverty*, what images come to mind? I think of those struggling, those with little food, clothing, or shelter. We live in a culture that glamorizes fame and wealth, and undermines poverty. It's easy to get wrapped up in the misconceptions of what poverty really means or is. When I started this study, I was lead to study Scripture on the words *poor* and *poverty* (and their variations). It has been fascinating. Here are just some of the definitions of poor and poverty that this study revealed: "needy, humble, weak, haggard, scrawny, afflicted, oppressed, low status, lack of resources, lean, barren, destitute, lack, scarcity, wicked, beggar, despised, miserable, having no or little social value."[1]

As I started to unravel these definitions, my heart began to sink. These words revealed to my heart the condition of the poor—oppressed, exploited, and afflicted. Before starting this book, I felt that if you were poor, then you needed to find a way out. I thought that if you wanted to change your circumstances, then you could, and everything else was just an excuse. But in time, I discovered that there are many poor in the world today who can't change their circumstances.

The United Nations refers to this as the *poverty trap*.[2] It is a generational, perpetual cycle of poverty. If this cycle isn't broken within a family, the majority of the family will be subject to living in poverty the rest of their lives. God calls us to bring justice to the poor, and we can do this by doing three things: empathizing with them, sharing with and giving resources to them, and raising them up. Let's discuss each of these.

Empathize

Living in the United States, as well as with those who live in many other developed countries or areas, it is hard to comprehend the magnitude of suffering that people undergo each day, hour, minute, and second. People are hungry and don't have proper shelter. People are sick, lack work, and scrounge by to make it to tomorrow. Perhaps many are heavy with fear, fearful that their children may die of starvation or fall victim to a deadly disease.

How many of us can truly grasp this way of living? The Word of God calls us to not overlook the poor. Yet in our comfortable environments, they can be easily missed. We tend to be more focused on the latest fashions while millions suffer from the pressures of poverty. Ultimately, it comes down to perspective. While not all of us are called to work in a ministry serving the needy for the rest of our lives, we are all called to give to and share with them (see 2 Cor. 9:6–15). And before we can genuinely share with and give to the poor, we must first empathize with them. Jesus empathized with the poor and commissioned us to become active participants in their lives.

"Be careful not to do your 'acts of righteousness' before men, to be seen by them. If you do, you will have no reward from your Father in heaven. So when you give to the needy, do not announce it with trumpets, as the hypocrites do in the synagogues and on the streets, to be honored by men. I tell you the truth, they have received their reward in full. But when you give to the needy, do not let your left hand know what your right hand is doing, so that your giving may be in secret. Then your Father, who sees what is done in secret, will reward you."
Matthew 6:1-4

"Then the King will say to those on his right, 'Come, you who are blessed by my Father; take your inheritance, the kingdom prepared for you since the creation of the world. For I was hungry and you gave me something to eat, I was thirsty and you gave me something to drink, I was a stranger and you invited me in, I needed clothes and you clothed me, I was sick and you looked after me, I was in prison and you came to visit me.' Then the righteous will answer him, 'Lord, when did we see you hungry and feed you, or thirsty and give you something to drink? When did we see you a stranger and invite you in, or needing clothes and clothe you? When did we see you sick or in prison and go to visit you?' The King will reply, 'I tell you the truth, whatever you did for one of the least of these brothers of mine, you did for me.'"
Matthew 25:34-40

Then Jesus said to his host, "When you give a luncheon or dinner, do not invite your friends, your brothers or relatives, or your rich neighbors; if you do, they may invite you back and so you will be

repaid. But when you give a banquet, invite the poor, the crippled, the lame, the blind, and you will be blessed. Although they cannot repay you, you will be repaid at the resurrection of the righteous."
Luke 14:12–14

Job also empathized with the poor in Job 24:1–12:

> Why does the Almighty not set times for judgment …
> Men move boundary stones; they pasture flocks they have stolen.
> They drive away the orphan's donkey and take the widow's ox in pledge.
> They trust the needy from the path and force all the poor of the land into hiding.
> Like wild donkeys in the desert, the poor go about their labor of foraging food; the wasteland provides food for their children.
> They gather fodder in the fields and glean in the vineyards of the wicked.
> Lacking clothes, they spend the night naked; they have nothing to cover themselves in the cold.
> They are drenched by mountain rains and hug the rocks for lack of shelter.
> The fatherless child is snatched from the breast; the infant of the poor is seized for a debt.
> Lacking clothes, they go about naked; they carry the sheaves, but still go hungry.
> They crush olives among the terraces; they tread the winepresses, yet suffer thirst.
> The groans of the dying rise from the city, and the souls of the wounded cry out for help. But God charges no one with wrong

doing.

Job's anguish for the poor is exemplified here; he is saddened by the oppression they continually undergo. While these words depict poverty in ancient history, this magnitude of poverty still exists in the world today. Here's an example from a blog written about those living in a trash dump outside of Tegucigalpa, Honduras:

> The children of the dump work as hard as the adults do. They have two main goals each day. The first is to fill large trash bags with as much plastic or paper as they can. Then, near to the end of the day, men drive into the dump with pick-up trucks and buy the bags full of recyclable material. The middle men usually pay fifty Honduran centavos per pound, or about three US cents. The kids can make a dollar on a good day. Their second goal? To find their breakfast, lunch and dinner among the trash.[3]

These children are stuck in a *poverty trap*. They are subject to these harsh conditions; it is all they have ever known. The United Nations confirms the hopelessness of these people's lives:

> People don't live in the squalor of the slums, favellas, squatter communities, low-rent districts or beside garbage dumps because they want to. They have no other choice.[4]

The United Nation depicts the poverty trap as a *vicious cycle* made up of several elements:

1. Poor health, disease and disability

2. Lack of education
3. Translating from generation to generation
4. Environments of social conflict[4]

So when you think of the poor, think about those in the poverty trap all around the world and those who have no other choice. Use the material presented here, coupled with your own research, to really understand the dire straits of those trapped in poverty. Then move in the Spirit to bless them as Jesus did.

Share and Give

According to the Sabbath laws presented in Exodus (23:10–11), the Israelites were told to leave their fields unplowed or unused in the seventh year so the poor could get food from them. They were instructed to do the same with their vineyards and olive groves—what a beautiful depiction of true philanthropy. By doing this, these farmers sacrificed profit in order to help the poor, yet ultimately their obedience yielded six strong years of production. These six strong years were from the Lord so that they might be able to bless the needy in the seventh year while also providing for their own families. Their obedience in sharing led to blessing.

Sharing with the needy from one's abundance was a commandment under the Mosaic Law. It is also a commission under the New Covenant (see 2 Corinthians 9:6–15). Sharing from the resources we've been blessed with falls into the "reap what you sow" concept. This central principle of God's heart has never gone away. Proverbs 22:9 states:

> A *generous* man will himself be blessed, for he shares his food with the poor. (Emphasis added.)

I love how the word *generous* is used in this passage. Generosity can be uncomfortable. And the Israelites gave up a portion of their profits in order to benefit the poor. I am sure that was uncomfortable for them, but their reverence for the Lord was stronger than their discomfort. It blessed them more in the end.

Generosity can require us to give up something we want, in light of God's prompting. One cannot fake generosity. God calls us to be generous with the poor. According to 2 Corinthians 9:6–15, this generosity is as simple as sharing with the needy. As we grow in our generosity, we "will be made rich in every way" so that we can be "generous on every occasion" (2 Cor. 9:11). This comes from our "generosity in sharing with them and everyone else" (2 Cor. 9:13). Generosity is tied to sharing. Sharing is hard, whether with siblings while growing up or with the poor as an adult. It is a form of maturity that we are all called to mold into as Christians.

Sometimes it can be hard to give *our* resources to those in need. We may find ourselves saying, "I hope this money is going where they say it is," or, "I want to give, but I don't have anything to give." These concerns are understandable. I believe there is a clear line in the sand between logic and generosity. Generosity is spurred on by the Spirit and at times may seem to defy logic. When we are generous, we glorify God. We exemplify His love for those we're giving to. This truth is made clear in 1 John 3:17, "If anyone has material possessions and sees his brother in need but has no pity on him, how can the love of God be in him?"

Raise Up

Anyone being raised up can't be oppressed at the same time. Oppression is the existence under one's thumb. It is demoralizing, hopeless, and agonizing. While many of the poor in the world today are oppressed, God will raise them up in time, despite what the world thinks. He will raise them up out of oppression and place them in seats of royalty (those who are redeemed by Jesus Christ):

> He raises the poor from the dust and lifts the needy from the ash heap; he seats them with princes, with the princes of their people. Psalm 113:7–8

We can collaborate with God in this effort. We have the opportunity to raise up the poor through our actions. In my studies, I found three ways we can raise up the poor: acknowledge them, protect them, and be a friend to them. Let's expand on each of these.

Acknowledge

Have you ever waved, smiled, or said hello to a stranger? Have you ever had that person not acknowledge you back? Isn't that a weird feeling? When this happens, most of us find ourselves either getting upset or hurt. We go into a tailspin: "What did I do?" or, "Do I have something in my teeth?" or, "What's his problem?" There is something powerful in acknowledgment that tugs at our souls.

There are many examples in the Bible of God calling upon His people to acknowledge Him. In order to receive Jesus into our hearts, we must acknowledge Him (see Matt. 10:32, 1 John 2:23). There is power in acknowledgment. And we can raise up the poor by acknowledging them.

Acknowledgment begins with awareness. So many of us hide from the poor. We don't support ministries that support the poor; we don't witness to the poor; we don't even make eye contact with them. I am just as guilty of these things at times. This may be because, for some of us, it is too uncomfortable, and for others perhaps it is judgment. Whatever it may be, our job starts with facing poverty head on. We must stop ignoring it. You can start today by making eye contact with someone in need. Smile at the person with warmth and love. Perhaps you may recognize a family in need at the grocery store and offer to buy them groceries. Acknowledgment brings dignity, which brings honor. This is the answer to love in 1 John 3:17.

Protect

Along with acknowledging the poor, we're called to protect them. Have you ever heard a mother say that she had to go *momma bear* on someone? Most of us have a core instinct to protect the weak (male or female). In regard to the *momma bear* example, this is because children are weak, innocent, and vulnerable. We want to protect them from danger and harm. This instinct is a form of justice. Because God calls us not to overlook the poor, we are called to protect them as well.

> Defend the cause of the weak and fatherless; maintain the rights of the poor and oppressed. Rescue the weak and needy; deliver them from the hand of the wicked.
> Psalm 82:3–4

> Stop doing wrong, learn to do right! Seek justice, encourage the oppressed. Defend the cause of the fatherless, plead the case of the widow.
> Isaiah 1:16–17

To protect the poor, we must be their voice when they don't have one.

Some excellent examples of this are ministries that work to educate children to get them out of poverty or ministries that counsel and shelter women who were slaves in sex trafficking. These organizations strive to bring dignity to those that society considers to be of little worth. They form a hedge of protection around these individuals in an effort to bring them out of their seemingly hopeless circumstances. These organizations are not just waiting for Jesus to return and for God to lift the needy out of the dung hill (Ps. 113:7), they are also making this a reality in the Kingdom today.

Be a Friend to the Poor
Last, we're called to be a friend to the poor. What does being a friend to the poor look like? Your core ability (true generosity) to be a friend to the poor is inspired by God. It is the love of God inside of you that desires to acknowledge someone who no one else does. It is the thread of justice that runs through your soul, desiring to protect the helpless from a world that seeks to swallow them up. Being a friend to the poor is a culmination of acknowledging and protecting them. It's putting our faith about what we've learned into action. Faith alone did not justify Abraham. His obedience (actions) did.

> You see that his faith and his actions were working together, and his faith was made complete by what he did. And the scripture was fulfilled that says, "Abraham believed God, and it was credited to him as righteousness," and he was called God's friend. You see that a person is justified by what he does and not by faith alone.
> James 2:22–24

To be a friend to the poor, we must act. And we must find a way to start today. This does not mean that we have to fly halfway around the world to bring water to the poor. You can also start today by reaching out to someone you know who is in need. Perhaps the Spirit will move you to reach out to someone you don't even know. Pray that the Lord places these people on your heart and that you will have the unwavering willingness to bless them, no matter the cost.

Chapter 4:
Understanding Wealth

Just as we're called to empathize with, share with, and raise up the poor, we're also called to better understand wealth and what it means in relation to the Kingdom of God. The way we think about wealth and how it's managed is just as important as our actions toward the poor. Wealth is a controversial subject within the Christian community; it shouldn't be. The Word of God is clear on the subject. As we get closer to the heart of God on all matters involving money, doubt will begin to fade.

In this chapter we will learn how to position our hearts toward wealth, what it looks like to cultivate it righteously and unrighteously, and how we are called to manage it. We will uncover why wealth is not a sin, but that corrupt motives to obtain it can be. When we are driven by greed, wealth is poisoned by greed. When we are driven by love, wealth is utilized for good.

In his book *Relentless*, John Bevere gives us a big-picture view of God's heart about wealth:

> For some reason, many people believe that godliness is exemplified by not having enough. In extreme cases, some people even take vows of poverty in their service for God. This mind-set fails in the face of Philippians 4:19, where Paul assures his Christian colleagues, "My God will liberally supply (fill to the full) your every need according to His riches in glory in Christ Jesus" (AMP).
>
> If you read that verse in context you will find that Paul is speak-

-ing to these believers specifically about finances. Based on this promise, we can be confident that it is God's will that you never lack any good thing. The psalmist writes, "The young lions lack food and suffer hunger, but they who seek (inquire of and require) the Lord [by right of their need and on the authority of His Word], none of them shall lack any beneficial thing" (Psalm 34:10, AMP). Lack and poverty are *not* life in all its fullness; therefore they cannot be God's will for your life.

The Scriptures declare that a good name is better than great riches or even the precious anointing of God (see Proverbs 22:1; Ecclesiastes 7:1). If we cannot pay our bills, we propagate a bad name.

From these scriptures, it appears that God's desire is to go further than just *meeting* our needs. It seems that He wants us to *prosper*. Hear His will in the apostle John's prayer: "Beloved, I wish *above all things* that thou mayest prosper and be in health, even as thy soul prospereth" (3 John 2, KJV).

God's will *above all things* is for you to prosper and be in good health. Amazing!

What is prosperity? It's having more than enough to meet not only *your* needs but also the needs of those in your world of influence. In other words, money should never be the deciding factor in whether you will reach out to the people God calls you to touch in His name.

God is not opposed to our having money. What He's against is money having us. Money is not the root of all evil; the *love of it* is. It is God's will for you to prosper in every area of life, even financially."[1]

In the past, I had the belief that wealth was not of God, and the desire for it was a sin; this perspective has changed. This chapter is written to those of you who either feel or have felt these things. While I don't think that all of us aspire to be wealthy, I do believe that deep down inside all of us there is a sense of *comfort* and *security* that wealth can bring. Because of this I think it is very important that we study wealth from God's perspective according to His Word. Once we better understand what God has to say about wealth, we can progress toward how He asks us to cultivate and manage it in a way that is glorifying to Him.

In an effort to discuss wealth from God's perspective, I have broken it into three areas: your heart's position toward wealth, how you can cultivate wealth righteously and unrighteously, and how you're called to manage wealth. First is your heart's position toward wealth. In order to better our relationship with wealth, we must first see it as God sees it. By looking at it from God's perspective, we can start seeing it for the good that it can do rather than fearing it because we think it's wrong.

Heart Position toward Wealth

You have your perceptions about wealth, and so do I. If you were to ask someone in poverty what wealth looks like, he or she might say it looks like the house you live in, the car you drive, and the clothes you wear. We all have different perceptions about wealth, but God's view on it does not shift. So the first matter we need to settle is how God asks us to view wealth. There are three stances God asks us to take about wealth: hold it loosely, don't focus on it solely, and know that it's fleeting.

Hold Wealth Loosely

We are called to hold all things in life loosely, including wealth. When we cultivate wealth, it is very hard not to grow attached to it. That's why it's so critical to get into a right relationship with it. Wealth can be comforting, empowering, and freeing. These are all things that the human spirit continually yearns for. While wealth can provide these things, it is important to remember the true provider of these things—God. While wealth can be a blessing, it is important not to root our identity in it. We must hold it loosely.

Keep Your Focus Right

Because wealth can provide the comfort, empowerment, and freedom that our souls crave, it is critical to keep a proper focus that does not live only *for* or *toward* it. A predator on our path toward proper focus is discontentment. Finding contentment in where we are today is key. While this is easier said than done, contentment can be found constantly by realigning our focus on the things that really matter. While the promise of wealth may bring a sense of rest and comfort to us, our focus must never be on it. While tempting, I challenge you instead to focus on the promises available to us through Jesus Christ. The fruit of this is contentment. First Timothy 6:6 states, "But godliness with contentment is great gain."

Ultimately, as Jesus said, "For where your treasure is, there your heart will be also" (Matt. 6:21). It is God's desire to protect us! If our treasure is rooted in wealth and we lose all of it to unforeseen circumstances, will we be OK with only Jesus? Focusing on wealth also produces a false sense of security. God gives us these principles in His Word to point us back to the fact that wealth is temporal, not eternal. As we work toward honoring God with our lives, we must remain neutral about the level of wealth we can amass. The goal is to reposition our focus to cultivating wealth that provides for our families and also blesses others. We move from amassing and hoarding to providing and blessing. A misaligned focus on wealth can lead to destruction.

> The wealth of the rich is their fortified city; they imagine it an unscalable wall.
> Proverbs 18:11

> Whoever loves money never has money enough; whoever loves wealth is never satisfied with his income.
> Ecclesiastes 5:10

> [W]ealth hoarded to the *harm* of its owner, or wealth *lost* through some misfortune.
> Ecclesiastes 5:13–14 (Emphasis added.)

When we long for wealth, our focus on God can get off track. A properly aligned focus can produce contentment because we're focused on Jesus.

Wealth Is Fleeting

By holding wealth and possessions loosely and not allowing them to envelop our lives, we can confidently stand in the reality that wealth is fleeting. Financial wealth can be cultivated during your lifetime. While it is not a sin to cultivate wealth, it becomes one if the pursuit of wealth consumes you.

Wealth should be a means to better the lives of those around us. It is our opportunity to give to others, while glorifying God in the process by directing the focus off ourselves and to God (see 2 Cor. 9). While we all have the ability to cultivate wealth here on earth, we must always remember it is fleeting.

> Naked a man comes from his mother's womb, and as he comes, so he departs. He takes nothing from his labor that he can carry in his hand.
> Ecclesiastes 5:15

Sometimes there is a tendency to associate wealth with God's blessing for *good behavior*. This misunderstanding can further add to the confusion about why God would bless evil people with wealth. Let's remember the overarching truth—we live in a world with free choice. Because we have free choice, there will always be those who prosper outside of moral means. As believers, we must remember it is God who ultimately gives us the ability to produce wealth (see Deut. 8:18). He also humbles and exalts the wealthy (see 1 Sam. 2:7). Therefore, it is important that we never build our identities to relate to our financial condition. If Paul had done that, then he wouldn't have had a ministry! It can be tempting to hinge our identities on our bank balances. This foundation is shaky. There are many components of wealth—esteem, position, success, and health. Yet all of these components are volatile and can crumble beneath us at any time.

> For all can see that the wise men die; the foolish and the senseless alike perish and leave their wealth to others.
> But man, despite his riches, does not endure; he is like the beasts that perish.
> This is the fate of those who trust in themselves, and of their followers, who approve their sayings.
> Like sheep they are destined for the grave, and death will feed on them.
> The upright will rule over them in the morning; their forms will

decay in the grave, far from their princely mansions.

But God will redeem my life from the grave; he will surely take me to himself.

Do not be overawed when a man grows rich, when the splendor of his house increases;

for he will take nothing with him when he dies, his splendor will not descend with him.

Though while he lived he counted himself blessed—and men praise you when you prosper—he will join the generations of his fathers, who will never see the light of life.

A man who has riches without understanding is like the beasts that perish.

Psalm 49:10, 12–20

Because wealth isn't eternal, it is ultimately out of our control. But we do have control over how our hearts are positioned toward it. We can also work toward cultivating and managing wealth in a way that glorifies God—this we have control over. By remembering these three areas in regard to how our hearts are positioned toward wealth, we start to see wealth as God sees it and to know that it is not wealth itself that is a sin.

Next we're going to talk about the cultivation of wealth. Wealth can be a tough topic because there are those who are morally good with it and those who are morally corrupt with it. There are also those who are evil and wealthy and those who are righteous and poor. In the Christian community, it seems that we continually demonize wealth. So how can we cultivate it in a way that is pleasing to the Father? This is what we're going to discuss next. The goal is to demystify the fear of cultivating wealth and to demonstrate that it can be obtained morally.

It comes back to what we are fueled by—greed or the desire to bless family and others.

Cultivating Wealth

Just as your heart's position toward wealth is critical, so also is the way you go about cultivating it. Many have amassed great wealth through shady dealings, but that does not mean that everyone who has wealth got there dishonestly.

Let's look at Abraham, who had great wealth. Genesis 12:1 states, "The Lord had said to Abram, 'Leave your country, your people and your father's household and go to the land I will show you.'" In the verses preceding these, the Lord begins to lay out all that He will bless Abraham with if he obeys. Verse 4 opens with these life-changing words, "So Abram left, as the Lord had told him…" As we read through the chapters that follow, we continue to see the unfolding of Abraham's faithfulness to and worship of the Lord. God blesses Abraham for his obedience. Abraham's obedience was real and sincere. It came from his heart.

Too many times I hear people say, "See what God did in Abraham's life? Pray this and it will happen for you, too!" They present a formula for wealth and use God's Word as the means to get there. God will not be mocked. There is no formula to crack His code. Abraham was not trying to plug certain steps into a formula to obtain wealth. Abraham's heart was pure, and he wanted to honor God in all he did. For his heart, devotion, and obedience, God blessed him. Obedience to God is the expressed translation of a believer's love toward God.

Naturally, this can raise the question, "What about the poor who are obedient to the Lord?" When we look at the poor widow in the gospels, we see a woman who was very poor but put "all she had to live on," into the offering (Mark 12:44). What about her? I do wish I had the answer to that question, but I don't. Perhaps I never will. What I do know is that Scripture calls us to use our means to bless others, whether our means are abundant or meager. This goes back to the prior chapter on poverty. The Scriptures command us not to turn a blind eye to the poor. The people of Sodom, in their abundance, turned a blind eye to the poor, and they were destroyed (Ezek. 16:49). Proverbs 28:27 states, "He who gives to the poor will lack nothing, but he who closes his eyes to them receives many curses."

So what about those of us who don't feel like we have anything to give? *Merriam-Webster* defines wealth as "a large amount of money and possessions, a value of all property, possessions and money that someone or something has, a large amount or number"[2]—*large*, the extra after our needs are provided for. A majority of us are considered wealthy; we have extra beyond our needs. So for those of us who feel like we have nothing to give, I am confident that if we can position our hearts toward generosity, then God will provide us with opportunities to give, no matter how meager our means may feel. While you may not have the desire to cultivate large amounts of wealth, God still calls all of us to be generous givers.

Cultivating wealth can be done unrighteously and righteously. Let's discuss these as they are laid out in Scripture to ensure that our labor glorifies the Father. But before we do, let's make sure that we avoid these big pitfalls as depicted in Scripture:

Haman *boasted* to them about his vast wealth.
Esther 5:11 (Emphasis added.)

"[W]oe to him who piles up stolen goods and makes himself

wealthy by *extortion*!"
Habakkuk 2:6 (Emphasis added.)

"Here now is the man who did not make God his stronghold but trusted in his great wealth and grew strong by *destroying* others!"
Psalm 52:7 (Emphasis added.)

By your great skill in trading you have increased your wealth, and because of your wealth your heart has *grown* proud.
Ezekiel 28:5 (Emphasis added.)

From these Scriptures we can see that it's not wealth or the cultivation of it that is a sin, but rather the motives. Cultivating wealth rooted in pride and greed will lead to destruction; these sins will poison your crop. This is why keeping your focus on God is critical. Let's review some different ways one can cultivate wealth as described in Scripture.

God's Blessing
God's financial blessing upon you is a blessing. The Scriptures remind us to "remember the Lord your God, for it is he who gives you the ability to produce wealth" (Deut. 8:18). Therefore, if we are wealthy, then we are blessed. To attribute our wealth to our sole efforts is ignorant and arrogant. God can remove wealth from our lives at any time. As we earlier learned in the definition of wealth, it can be defined as the *large* amount of something. The majority of the time, that large amount of something consists of extra. Wealth does not always translate into a mansion or luxury car; it is extra of something beyond what we *need*.

Isaac planted crops in that land and the same year reaped a

hundredfold, because *the Lord blessed him*. The man became rich, and his wealth continued to grow until he became very wealthy.
Genesis 26:12-13 (Emphasis added.)

The blessing of the Lord brings wealth, and he adds no trouble to it.
Proverbs 10:22 (Emphasis added.)

Inheritance

An inheritance is a blessing of wealth. When we read the Scriptures, we do see that wealth was passed down through families for multiple generations and it was an honorable way to bless those you love.

> Houses and wealth are inherited from parents.
> Proverbs 19:14

> Blessed is the man who fears the Lord, who finds great delight in his commands. His children will be mighty in the land; the generation of the upright will be blessed. Wealth and riches are in his house, and his righteousness endures forever.
> Psalm 112:1–3

> Jesus continued: "There was a man who had two sons. The younger one said to his father, 'Father, give me my share of the estate.' So he divided his property between them."
> Luke 15:11–12

> Abraham left everything he owned to Isaac.
> Genesis 25:5

So if you receive wealth (extra) through an inheritance, consider it a blessing.

Hard Work

Hard work contributes to wealth (see Prov. 10:4). It is important to remember that beyond hard work, we cannot attribute success to our hard work alone. We must steer clear of pride when working to cultivate wealth. There is nothing wrong with working hard to provide for family and making a better life, yet we must remember who gives us the ability to do so:

> You may say to yourself, "My power and the strength of my hands have produced this wealth for me." But remember the Lord your God, for it is he who gives you the ability to produce wealth.
> Deuteronomy 8:17–18

Remain vigilant about being overly confident in your ability to produce wealth and thus eliminating your reliance on God (see 1 Sam. 2:7).

With all of this said, I believe **God blesses those who move in obedience to Him.**

We simply can't sit still and do nothing for Him and the Kingdom and then cry out for Him to bless us. God requires us to move in obedience to Him.

Position of Authority

Throughout history and even today, wealth is often associated with those who are in a position of authority. While some in power don't handle themselves in a way that glorifies Christ, I would say that wealth is a natural by-product of most authority positions.

Jesus entered Jericho and was passing through. A man was there by the name of Zacchaeus; he was *a chief tax collector* and was wealthy.
Luke 19:1-2 (Emphasis added.)

The Lord established the Kingdom *under his control*; and all Judah brought gifts to Jehoshaphat, so that he had great wealth and honor.
2 Chronicles 17:5 (Emphasis added.)

David son of Jesse was *king over all Israel.* He ruled over Israel forty years—seven in Hebron and thirty-three in Jerusalem. He died at a good old age, having enjoyed long life, wealth and honor.
1 Chronicles 29:26-28 (Emphasis added.)

King Xerxes reigned from his royal throne…For a full 180 days he displayed the vast wealth of his kingdom and the splendor and glory of his majesty.
Esther 1:2, 4 (Emphasis added.)

"Now then, I tell you the truth: Three more *kings* will appear in Persia, and then a fourth, who will be far richer than all the others."
Daniel 11:2 (Emphasis added.)

A certain *ruler* asked him, "Good teacher, what must I do to inherit eternal life?" [Jesus] said to him, "Sell everything you have and give to the poor." When he heard this, he became very sad because he was a man of great wealth.
Luke 18:18, 22-23 (Emphasis added.)

Extortion and Oppression

An example of cultivating wealth dishonestly is doing so via dishonest scales through extortion or oppression. Since God is good, cultivating wealth through extortion or oppression is not of Him. Most of us read this and think to ourselves, "I would never do that!" Maybe you wouldn't steal the shirt off a homeless man's back, but dishonest scales can be measured in less obvious forms. Here's an example:

> You're getting ready to sell your house and there is a mold problem. The home inspector didn't find it. In order for you to address this issue, you have to shell out $10,000. Are you going to hide the problem in order to hold onto the $10,000?

These *little white lies* become a form of extortion or oppression. Dictonary.com defines a white lie as, "a minor, polite, or harmless lie; fib."[3] When did lies become minor, polite, and harmless?

> "You belong to your father, the devil, and you want to carry out your father's desire. He was a murderer from the beginning, not holding to the truth, for there is no truth in him. When he lies, he speaks his native language, for he is a liar and the father of lies."
> John 8:44

> "But the cowardly, the unbelieving, the vile, the murderers, the sexually immoral, those who practice magic arts, the idolaters and all liars—their place will be in the fiery lake of burning sulfur. This is the second death."
> Revelation 21:8

There is no such thing as a *white lie*.

Lies are not innocent, and they are not of God because they originate from the devil. Anytime anyone lies to protect money, gain more of it, or obtain something he or she wants, he or she is not acting in accordance with God.

> "Woe to him who piles up stolen goods and makes himself wealthy by extortion!"
> Habakkuk 2:6

> He who oppresses the poor to increase his wealth and he who gives gifts to the rich—both come to poverty.
> Proverbs 22:16

> Do not exploit the poor because they are poor and do not crush the needy in court, for the Lord will take up their case and will plunder those who plunder them.
> Proverbs 22:22–23

> "The people of the land practice extortion and commit robbery; they oppress the poor and needy and mistreat the alien, denying them justice."
> Ezekiel 22:29

It is honorable for believers to cultivate wealth by noble means, but lying and oppressing others to gain wealth is sinful. There is no such thing as a white lie in an effort to gain the things that we want. A lie is a lie in the eyes of God.

Part of ensuring that our hearts are in the right place for cultivating wealth entails an examination of motives. Our motives can be rooted in a focus on ourselves or on God.

Motives Check

Because money is the fuel for our ministries and the funds for so many other things like sending missionaries overseas, the needs of families, the needs of the poor, and so much more, it is critical that we're focused on God. If we're focused on God, then wealth can become a natural progression in our lives (not always). If we're focused on wealth, then it can still come, but it will never seem to be enough. So the question is, "Where am I focused?"

Focused on Self

When we're focused on ourselves, it is all about how much wealth we can amass to prove to the world who we are and who we've become! The pursuit of wealth can also be about *pleasure*, yet the heart issue lies in our desire to *prove* to others who we are through wealth. I picture it like this:

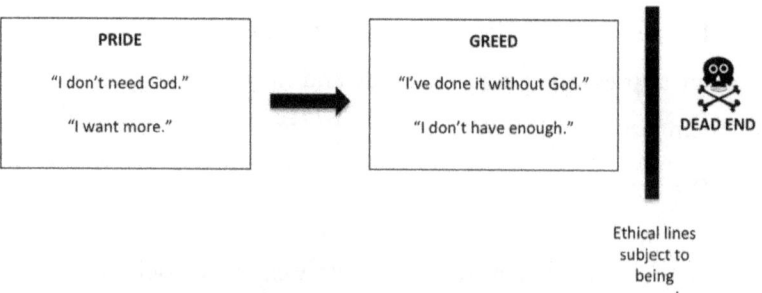

Ethical lines subject to being crossed.

While this illustration does not cover all sinful motives, use it as a guide to direct yourself to your motives. By determining your motives, you can determine what is driving your focus. **Don't allow prideful**

ignorance to stand in the way of identifying where your heart stands.

When we are focused solely on wealth, we are driven by pride, which can then lead to greed. Some of us have dreamed about the fruit of selfish wealth, which thrives on building a bigger and better empire. When we are there, we run the risk of being driven by emotions that are fueled by greed, which usually leads to ethical lines being crossed in order to acquire more.

Focused on God

As we're cultivating wealth, the fruit is much sweeter if we're focused on God. Again, it's not that wealth is bad, but a wrong focus can be. When we think about building wealth, we need to let it be a natural progression of obedience to our Father, which in turn we can use for good. When we're focused on God and our attitudes and actions are in obedience to Him, the product of our altered focus becomes eternal:

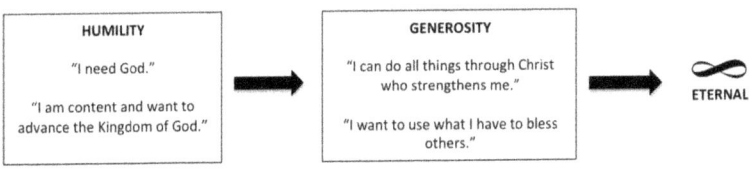

Management of Wealth

The way that we manage wealth is an excellent representation of our motives and attitudes in regard to money. As Randy Alcorn says in *The Law of Rewards*, "Our handling of money is a litmus test of our true character."[4] When most of us hear about the management of wealth, we think of investments and budgets. While those items do fall into this category, we are going to address it from a heart perspective. The way we manage our children and our households stems from our hearts. The way we speak to our spouses stems from our hearts. The way we drive down the road and treat other people stems from our hearts. All actions and words are rooted in our hearts. The management of our wealth is the culmination of our motives and resources coming together. I believe that beyond managing our wealth in a wise way, we are additionally called to humbly manage it. Our spirits undergo many stages of growth in life, and in growth we all experience a sense of pride and humility. Proverbs 16:18 says that, "Pride goes before destruction, a haughty spirit before a fall."

All of us who have the means to cultivate wealth can nobly do so, yet that is not the end of the journey. Growth entails stages of humility in our persistence, but also we must avoid arrogance in our success. This becomes more important than picking the next best investment.

> Humility and the fear of the Lord bring wealth and honor and life.
> Proverbs 22:4

Humility as defined by *Merriam-Webster* is "the quality or state of not thinking you are better than other people."[5] In Proverbs 22:4, the Hebrew word for humility, *nawa*, is defined as to "stoop down."[6] Humility is the exact opposite of pride. While wealth is not sinful, an incorrect view of it can be. This view can be one of pride or even laziness cloaked in a false spirit of humility. As Christians, we are empowered by God's grace to do great things! John 14:12 says that whoever believes in Jesus Christ will do the works he did, and even greater! We are called to press forward in our callings and not be afraid—even of wealth. Wealth is never guaranteed, but we should never fear it. God can utilize a generous believer to bless many lives.

By having a healthy heart position toward wealth, cultivating it morally, and managing it humbly, we can stand confident in our beliefs. We have the opportunity to inspire other believers to see wealth for what it can do and to come together to join around missions that advance God's Kingdom and glorify Him! I do hope that this chapter has helped you to clarify controversial topics on wealth. I also pray that you can utilize this information to dig deeper in your own studies.

In the next chapter, we'll start to uncover that while poverty is not a sin; to proclaim that it is God's will for every Christian is *false*.

Chapter 5:
The Lack of Nobility in Poverty

The goal of this chapter is *not* to reveal poverty as a sin, but to debunk the myth that it's God's will for all Christians to be poor or perhaps that wealth might corrupt a believer's relationship with God. The truth is that there is no nobility in poverty. God favors neither poverty nor wealth. And even perhaps in a state of poverty, when provided with ample opportunities to pull ourselves out, we risk not contributing to the advancement of God's Kingdom as we should. So we move toward a concern of mine—why do so many Christians believe that God wants them to be poor or that only in poverty we can honor Him? I hope that from what you've studied so far, you can see that this belief is not congruent with the Word.

Many of us have been taught that money is the root of all evil, and we should avoid it at all costs. Some of us have even taken a vow of poverty by living ascetic lives in an effort to glorify God. While the pursuit of working toward pleasing the Father is a noble cause, I don't see one in poverty.

The belief that God favors the poor is derived from many verses sprinkled throughout the Bible. An example of one is found in James 2:5–7:

> Listen, my dear brothers: Has not God chosen those who are poor in the eyes of the world to be rich in faith and to inherit the kingdom he promised those who love him? But you have insulted the poor. Is it not the rich who are exploiting you? Are they not the

ones who are dragging you into court? Are they not the ones who are slandering the noble name of him to whom you belong?

If this verse—along with 1 Timothy 6:10, "For the love of money is a root of all kinds of evil"—were the only Scriptures you ever heard preached about money, it would be understandable why you might think that money is bad and that nobility is found in poverty.

Before studying biblical financial stewardship, I, too, believed that if God wanted us to have money, then He would make it happen. My foundation was that too much money is bad, money is the root of all evil, and God favors the poor. I struggled with the thought of making too much money and appearing wealthy. A lot of Christians struggle with these concerns; they ask what kind of house is acceptable to live in or what kind of car is OK to drive. You will never be able to get the answers to these questions from someone else. The answers need to come from your heart; these matters are between you and God.

James 2:5-7 tends to be taken out of context, along with 1 Timothy 6:10. Take a moment and read James 2:1-13; you will find that these verses are about not favoring anyone, ever. James is urging these church leaders to quit favoring the rich over the poor. In verses 8 and 9, he speaks out against favoring anyone. If we are being instructed here not to favor the rich over the poor, why then would God turn around and tell us to favor the poor over the rich? Favoritism of any sort is forbidden. God is not in favor of either one, but He certainly stands against us being in favor of one over the other.

We cannot fear money for the angst of being dissuaded by the comfort of it. Money can bring comfort, empowerment, and freedom. If our hearts are in the right place (rooted in Christ and not in money) and we seek to bless the lives of others, money becomes a vehicle for a plethora of opportunities to bless others. Too many of us today remain in a financial condition where we are struggling to get by. For some of us, this way of functioning is fueled by misguided information. As mentioned in the prior chapter, the world looks to Christians to be different. If the majority of us are stressed out and broke, how much of Christ are we really reflecting to the world? Why do so many of us operate under the pretense that "God will take care of me." Yes, Scripture is clear that God will provide for our every need, but that is not going to happen by just expecting Him to be our ATM. In order to have money, we have to work for it. There is no other way around this. Therefore, in order not to be poor, we have to make the decision (when we have the opportunity to change our circumstances) not to be poor. Nowhere in Scripture does it state that the poor are any better than the rich. If you have the opportunity to change your circumstances, then do it—no more excuses to stay poor because poverty is all you have ever known. To me, that is like saying alcoholism is a generational curse in your family, and it is all your family has ever known, so you are bound by it. Tough luck. What? Really—is this where we stop? I am an advocate for the poorest of the poor in this world, and it is my passion to utilize the resources that God has blessed me with to help them. These individuals are caught in a cycle of generational poverty that is, to most, *unbreakable*. But for the rest of us, what's our excuse?

We are subject to the world's system; we must recognize money is what makes the world go around—not literally, but I am sure you follow. While it does take money to make things move in this world, *we* are not always the *source* of it. Many of us have been blessed by others who felt directed by God to give to us. There are even supernatural circumstances through which God can provide.

I will never forget how God exemplified this in my life. He's inter-

-vened many times, but one story stands out. When I was nineteen years old, I was working as a waitress. While income was sufficient, it did fluctuate. There was a month that my income was really down. It was the night before my rent was due, and I realized that I was short. I cried out to God. I had no idea what to do. I had to have $350 by the next day, but I only had $230. The next morning came. As my roommate was running out the apartment, she grabbed a note posted to the door. She opened the note and read it aloud. It was from the office; they were notifying us that their system reflected that our account had a credit of $240. This credit split in half was the amount I was short! We were baffled. How did this *mysterious* credit show up in their system? We never overpaid our rent. We called the office and practically argued with them that their system was incorrect, but they said that there was nothing they could do because it was managed on a corporate level. They could not identify where the credit came from. It just happened to reflect a credit that morning. I told my roommate the story about how I prayed the night prior. I don't remember telling anyone about being short that month, except for God the night before. God answered my prayer—supernatural provision!

From this story, I came to know the following things about God and His faithfulness to us when we're in need. First, God can do the impossible (always believe Him for that). Second, God provides just as His Word says He will (Phil. 4:19). Third, money is necessary. It took money (electronic money anyway) to make the credit.

God will provide for us, but He still uses money from other sources to do it. Money is necessary. If we are caught in a perpetual cycle of fear regarding money, then our minds will be crippled. By gaining a proper understanding of money, we will have the strength to propel the Kingdom of God forward. If I had to deal with being short for rent every month, I cannot see how I would be able to effectively reflect God's love to others. We can't reflect the joy of God and give to others if we're stressed out about money all the time. There are going to be situations, rich or poor, when we need to look to God first. This further emphasizes that money is a heart issue, not a money issue. God does and will supernaturally come through in situations. Yet it does not mean that He is just sitting there waiting to perform miracle after miracle while we do nothing. We are called to be more than just a mouthpiece of faith-provoking stories. This supernatural experience did not happen to me solely so that I could only share it with you and others. It also happened to spur me on to more: to trust God with bigger and better things! Any effort to advance God's Kingdom on earth is backed by money. In order for you to fulfill the calling that God has on your life, you will require money. In order for your church to stay operating and open to the public, it will require money. In order for your city's roads to be maintained, they will require money. In order to keep the lights on in your house and the water running, it will require money. We need money to survive. We need extra money to advance forward.

Advancing Forward

One night Stephen and I were talking about the possibility of freed-up cash flow in the future. Freeing up cash flow is huge because in turn, you can use that extra cash toward debt-reduction, savings, and growth. In our conversation, I shared with Stephen that I wanted to ensure that we don't consume the extra money, but instead apply it toward savings and growth. I wanted to ensure that this cash flow would go toward advancing our mission. We agreed this cash was for the future and not to be consumed for immediate pleasure.

The same is true in regard to our mission in life or anything we are working toward *advancing*. There will always be the essentials. There is nothing wrong with the essentials, and we are called to be content with the essentials. But, in order to really make an impact, we need to work toward more than the essentials. These efforts should not be in vain or to build bigger and better empires necessarily, but to advance the mission that God has placed on our hearts. Simply working to provide for our needs, merely scraping by, frankly seems selfish and shortsighted. Where is God in that attitude? Just as much as the sole pursuit of wealth can be selfish, so can remaining in the mentality that poverty is noble.

When Jesus tells the rich young ruler to "sell your possessions and give to the poor…Come, follow me" (Matt. 19:21), he was not saying, "Your wealth is bad; get rid of it—it's holding you back." He was saying, "Focusing on your wealth is holding you back from fully serving me. Stop focusing on your stuff and start focusing on me." The Scripture says that "when the young man heard this, he went away sad, because he had great wealth" (Matt. 19:22). The word for wealth, *ktema*, used in Matthew 19:22 when translated back to the Greek is defined as "wealth, possessions, property, fields."[1] This guy had a lot of stuff, and he didn't want to part with it. If we go back, his initial question to Jesus was, "Teacher, what good thing must I do to get eternal life?" After Jesus responds to him, he asks, "What do I still lack?" (Matt. 19:16, 20). This is when Jesus reveals to him that he still lacks the ability to part with his stuff. This story has nothing to do with wealth being bad, as some interpret. This story cautions us against focusing too much on our stuff and becoming attached to it. When we become attached to our stuff, Jesus takes a backseat in our lives. We should never aspire to amass wealth so that we can stockpile more stuff. This is where the heart issue becomes prevalent. The stuff then *stuffs* the holes of our hearts instead of Jesus filling these holes. God created us with these holes in our hearts so that only Jesus can fill them to satisfaction.

Let's look at the parable of the rich fool. Before Jesus tells the parable, he states, "Watch out! Be on your guard against all kinds of greed; a man's life does not consist in the abundance of his possessions" (Luke 12:15). The term greed used here, *pleonexia*, is defined as "avarice,"[2] which is defined as "extreme greed for wealth or material gain."[3]

The parable of the rich fool is all about a man stockpiling the abundance of his crop for *himself*. This story has nothing to do with the fact that wealth or saving is bad—it has everything to do with two clear warnings from Jesus:

1. "Watch out! Be on your guard against all kinds of greed; a man's life does not consist in the abundance of his possessions."
Luke 12:15

2. "This is how it will be with anyone who stores up things for himself but is not rich toward God."
Luke 12:21

If we continue to read in Luke 12, we see the instructions of Christ not to worry about tomorrow and that God will provide for us. Later in verses 33-34, he says, "Sell your possessions and give to the poor. Provide purses for yourselves that will not wear out, a treasure in heaven that will not be exhausted, where no thief comes near and no moth destroys. For where your treasure is, there your heart will be also." These are the words of Jesus after he tells the parable of the rich fool, who was attached to his possessions—his crops. The rich fool's crops and barns are rotted into the ground now. In these verses, Jesus commissions us to stop stockpiling earthly possessions that rot and to invest in His Kingdom instead. We can utilize our resources to invest in a new boat or to advance the mission of Christ here on earth. I am not saying that investing in a boat is ungodly; I am saying **make sure that if you stockpile possessions here on earth, it is not in an effort to fill any holes in your heart**. Make sure that you are not missing out on investing in eternal treasure that won't rot.

Building up wealth beyond our everyday expenses is not ungodly. I believe ungodliness comes in when we handle our abundance incorrectly. The word abundance can be defined as "a very large quantity of something."[4] An abundance of something can be anything! In the case of the rich fool, it was an abundance of crops; and for the rich young ruler, it was an abundance of stuff. Joseph's life is a portrayal of how utilizing an abundance of blessings can in turn bless others. Joseph had the ability to interpret Pharaoh's dreams. After Joseph interpreted one of Pharaoh's dreams and warned him of an impending famine, he was put "in charge of the whole land of Egypt" (Gen. 41:41). Pharaoh also gave Joseph his signet ring and "dressed him in robes of fine linen" and made him "second-in-command" (Gen. 41:42–43).

> During the seven years of abundance the land produced plentifully. Joseph collected all the food produced in those seven years of abundance in Egypt and stored it in the cities. In each city he put the food grown in the fields surrounding it. Joseph stored up huge quantities of grain, like the sand of the sea; it was so much that he stopped keeping records because it was beyond measure. The seven years of abundance in Egypt came to an end, and the seven

years of famine began, just as Joseph had said. There was famine in all the other lands, but in the whole land of Egypt there was food. When the famine had spread over the whole country, Joseph opened the storehouses and sold grain to the Egyptians, for the famine was severe throughout Egypt. And all the countries came to Egypt to buy grain from Joseph, because the famine was severe in all the world.
Genesis 41:47–59

In this story, Joseph *stores up* resources to provide for his needs and also the needs of others. There is an amazing progression that takes place in this story, all leading to a clear portrayal of how to manage our abundance:

- God had a calling over Joseph's life in the midst of his trials.
- God gave Joseph a spiritual gifting so that he could fulfill his calling and help others.
- God gave Joseph *the favor* of men to execute his calling, in order to help the people.
- God gave Joseph insight and blessed the land so that Egypt could store up the necessary crops for the famine (abundance).
- Joseph stored up the crops.
- The crops were stored up (the abundance of) to bless others and help those in need.
- Joseph was obedient, thus bringing God glory.

Was Joseph wrong for "storing up abundance" in this story? No! Why? The reason is because he was not storing up the crops for himself (like the rich fool), but rather to help not only himself but also those in need. God blessed Joseph with authority and wealth so that he could execute this operation successfully. He used his wealth and power to bless others, not extort them. If Joseph was not given his unique gifting and if he had not gained Pharaoh's favor, then he would have remained locked up in the dungeon, never to fulfill his destiny! Do you really think that God is calling us to sit in a dungeon the rest of our lives? No way. Just like Joseph, you and I have a calling on our lives, and God desires to give us favor in the eyes of men, even in the midst of adversity.

> And God is able to make all grace abound to you, so that in all things at all times, having all you need, you will abound in every good work. As it is written: "He has scattered abroad his gifts to the poor; his righteousness endures forever." Now he who supplies seed to the sower and bread for food will also supply and increase your store of seed and will enlarge the harvest of your righteousness. You will be made rich in every way so that you can be generous on every occasion, and through us your generosity will result in thanksgiving to God. This service that you perform is not only supplying the needs of God's people but is also overflowing in many expressions of thanks to God. Because of the service by which you have proved yourselves, men will praise God for the obedience that accompanies your confession of the gospel of Christ, and for your generosity in sharing with them and with everyone else. And in their prayers for you their hearts will go out to you, because of the surpassing grace God has given you. Thanks be to God for his indescribable gift!
> 2 Corinthians 9:8–15

Let these verses be your new mission statement for how God is calling you to manage the resources under your care. God does not call us to be rich or poor; He has no favorites. But what He does call all of us to is a life of service and generosity. In order to serve in anything to our fullest capacity, we must first understand the inner workings of our duties. While I don't know your personal calling, I do know that God calls you to be a good manager of the resources He has entrusted to you. Not only does He call you to seek out understanding, but also He requires you to act. So step out in faith and move forward. This is a move only we can make.

As we move from the understanding that there is no nobility in being broke, we must further advance forward in action. You have already done this by reading this book. Great! Now I further encourage you to seek out all of the Bible verses we cover so that you better understand the context around them. I encourage you to get out a concordance and look up the words *money*, *rich*, *poor*, *wealth*, *generosity*, and the like. If there is one subject in life we should be schooled in, it is money. The way we view and manage money has a direct influence on so many aspects of our lives. This then translates into how we conduct ourselves, which in the end, we will be judged for. The closer we get to the truth, the freer we become. Study the Word of God on a deeper level in regard to this subject, and I am confident that your eyes will be opened. We must study this subject for ourselves so that we can stand confidently before God.

Ask yourself, in relation to biblical financial management, where does my teaching originate? If from someone else and you have not taken the time to fully study and know this topic yourself, the time is now. The words that you speak about this matter, and all matters, deeply affect the lives of those you oversee. While the lessons you teach on other aspects of life are very important, if your understanding about money is skewed, then you propagate that in the lives of those you serve.

Too many of us live trapped in lies relating to finances because we have not studied the Word for ourselves. Use this book to guide you, your leadership, and church members to a *clearer* understanding of how God views money, but then also learn how to manage it in a way that honors Him.

As Paul bids farewell in Acts 20, he says:

> Keep watch over yourselves and all the flock of which the Holy Spirit has made you overseers. Be shepherds of the church of God, which he bought with his own blood. I know that after I leave, savage wolves will come in among you and will not spare the flock. Even from your own number men will arise and distort the truth in order to draw away disciples after them. So be on your guard! In everything I did, I showed you that by this kind of hard work we must help the weak, remembering the words the Lord Jesus himself said: "It is more blessed to give than to receive."
> Acts 20:28–31, 35

Paul is pleading with tears in his eyes, pleading because he could foresee the magnitude of the masses being misled by the misguided.

Paul urges us to protect those we serve and to resist laziness in regard to what is being taught in our churches. We are responsible for protecting not only our calling, but also the calling of those under our care (see 1 Peter 5:2–3). Part of this is to fully understand what the Bible has to say about money and in turn to share those truths with the people you serve. Your church members want to make good decisions regarding money, but most don't know where to start. And most crave this guidance from the pulpit. They don't crave sermons on *tithing* but rather on the heart matters of money. The enemy is having a heyday in this area, and the further he can lead us astray in regard to God's truth, the less impact we will have on the Kingdom.

As you read this book and study on your own, address beliefs that are not congruent with the Word, such as "nobility in poverty." If this belief is in your heart, then it will come out in your sermons, thus affecting those you serve. Work to get to the core of God's heart on these topics so that His truths will be reflected in your life, setting others free!

Chapter 6:
Handling Wealth Generously

In the pursuit of debunking myths about the nobility in poverty, I direct you toward the pursuit of cultivating an abundance that not only provides for you and your family, but also advances the Kingdom of God.

When we have an abundance, we are called to manage it in a way that glorifies the Father. The primary way we can do this is by handling it generously. The first thing that we must accept is that an abundance is a gift from God:

> Moreover, when God gives any man wealth and possessions, and enables him to enjoy them, to accept his lot and be happy in his work—this is a gift of God.
> Ecclesiastes 5:19

The word *gift* here translates back to the Hebrew word *mattat*, which is defined as, "something given."[1] Wealth is a gift from God that we should handle in a way that glorifies Him. One way we can do this is by exhibiting generosity. By handling our resources generously, we in turn reflect the heart of God to others. Generosity cannot be faked. It is prompted by the Spirit and originates in the heart. Generosity is a stance we need to work toward so that as we cultivate our resources to create an abundance so we can honor the words of Jesus in Luke 12:48, "Everyone who has been given much, much will be demanded; and from the one who has been entrusted with much, much more will be asked." As we move toward cultivating an abundance, we must keep our focus properly aligned on God so that it does not become our *sole* focus.

It is important to remember that money possesses no moral bias. It is simply a medium of exchange. The *moral* structure of money never changes; it is only in the hands of the beholder, that money can assume a moral slant.

Handling abundance (the extra above our needs) generously requires a mature frame of mind. Maturity is not about having half the Bible memorized. Maturity in regard to an abundance is pressing into the heart of God as it pertains to money. It is about handling money in a way that glorifies God. You may be thinking, "Well, this is great, but I will worry about all of this when I actually cultivate wealth. Until then, I won't." I challenge this as unwise thinking. I would liken this thought process to signing up to run a marathon and not training for it. While you may be able to run the race, your body would probably go into shock. The same is true as we prepare to handle our finances in a way that glorifies God. We have to continually train our minds to handle what the Lord has prepared for us. Since money is an element that will always be necessary for survival, we need to figure out how to handle it starting *now*. God has placed resources within your grasp today, resources that He is calling you to manage and manage well.

Luke 16:10 says that "whoever can be trusted with very little can also be trusted with much, and whoever is dishonest with very little will also be dishonest with much." We have been entrusted with the ability to make wise decisions about how we handle abundance, which some of us possess now.

Later in Luke 16, Jesus cautions about the danger of trying to love both God and money:

"No servant can serve two masters. Either he will hate the one and love the other, or he will be devoted to the one and despise the other. You cannot serve both God and Money." The Pharisees, who loved money, heard all this and were sneering at Jesus. He said to them, "You are the ones who justify yourselves in the eyes of men, but God knows your hearts. What is highly valued among men is detestable in God's sight."
Luke 16:13–15

The first step to handling abundance properly is to understand what money is and not to place the cultivation of it in front of our devotion to God. An area that I have personally wrestled with is the question, "When is enough...enough?" Here are some examples:

- Is a $400,000 house too much?
- Is it OK to drive a luxury car?
- Is it OK to send my children to private school?
- Is flying business class too pretentious?
- Is it OK to vacation for four weeks?
- Is making over $100,000 per year too much?

This book will not answer these questions for you. These are what I call *heart matters*. *No one on earth* can answer these questions for you. These are between you and God. Instead, let me present a suggested thought process, bringing you through Scripture in an effort to settle your heart. Let's examine the lives of two men in the Bible, Abraham and King Solomon. Both had vast amounts of wealth, and from their stories, we will pull out lessons we can apply to these questions in an effort to give us direction. Let's start with King Solomon.

King Solomon

King Solomon is considered to be one of the wisest men that ever lived. He was the second son of David and Bathsheba, and Israel's third king, ruling for forty years during the golden age.² His story starts out in 1 Kings 3, when he becomes king and marries Pharaoh's daughter. While God knew that the Pharaoh's daughter would shift Solomon's focus away from Him to other gods, He still allowed Solomon to marry her.

In 1 Kings 3:5, we read that, "at Gibeon the Lord appeared to Solomon during the night in a dream, and God said, 'Ask for whatever you want me to give you.'" While Solomon could have asked for *anything*, he simply asked for "a discerning heart to govern your people and to distinguish between right and wrong" (1 Kings 3:9). With this answer the Lord was pleased and He responded to Solomon:

> "Since you have asked for this and not for long life or wealth for yourself, nor have asked for the death of your enemies but for discernment in administering justice, I will do what you have asked. I will give you a wise and discerning heart, so that there will never have been anyone like you, nor will there ever be. Moreover, I will give you what you have not asked for—both riches and honor—so that in your lifetime you will have no equal among kings. And if you walk in my ways and obey my statues and commands as David your father did, I will give you a long life."
> 1 Kings 3:11–14

Jerold Aust's article in *The Good News* points out that "these gifts from God required something: Solomon's resolute obedience to Him."³ Notice how Aust uses the word *gifts*. Not only did these gifts from God include wisdom, but also riches and honor! The Lord knew that if Solomon did not obey Him in the midst of his wealth and wisdom, then pride and other sin had a large door to enter into Solomon's heart.

For many years, King Solomon did obey the Lord in his ways. Part of this was building the temple that David was not able to complete during his lifetime. As the Lord had promised, King Solomon's wealth continued to grow. Upon the Queen of Sheba's visit, she exclaimed, "The report I heard in my own country about your achievements and your wisdom is true. But I did not believe these things until I came and saw with my own eyes. Indeed, not even half was told me; in wisdom and wealth you have far exceeded the report I heard" (1 Kings 10:6–7). Aust points out that the 666 talents of gold that King Solomon received each year as mentioned in verse 14 was equivalent to over $700 million today. The wealth that the Lord continued to allow Solomon to cultivate was great.

No where in God's words to Solomon did He say that wealth and possessions were bad or evil. God actually condoned King Solomon having these things and wanted to give them to him as a blessing. The trouble for Solomon came in the midst of the blessing when his heart began to shift away from God. Aust comments on this shift:

> But the king eventually showed a weakness that caused him to turn from the great God who blessed him. His wealth became so great, his fame so widespread, that he lost his *focus*. He became more and more attached to his physical surroundings, more dependent on his wealth, and more attentive to his many wives than he was to God.[3] (Emphasis added.)

This story clearly points to the fact that it was not King Solomon's wealth that was his downfall, but his disobedience in the midst of the blessing. Solomon started to disregard the warning of the Lord against intermarrying (1 Kings 11:2). King Solomon fell to his love for "many foreign women besides Pharaoh's daughter" (1 Kings 11:1), thus contaminating his marriage bed. Eventually Solomon had seven hundred wives and three hundred concubines and they led his heart astray (1 Kings 11:3). In the end, the Lord preserved Solomon's wealth and reign during his lifetime but only for the sake of his father, David, who kept the Lord's commandments (1 Kings 11:34).

Abraham

Abraham was also a man of great wealth (Gen. 13:2), but unlike Solomon, he was a man of great and lasting obedience (Gen. 26:5). Abraham's story of obedience began when the Lord told Abraham (at that time called Abram) to "leave your country, your people and your father's household and go to the land I will show you" (Gen. 12:1). For Abraham's obedience, the Lord promised him many blessings. During Abraham's continued obedience to the Lord throughout his life, he "became very wealthy in livestock and in silver and gold" (Gen. 13:2). During his lifetime, Abraham acted out of fear (Gen. 12:10-20) and impatience (Gen.16:1-4), and yet due to his persistent obedience, he was blessed and so were the generations after him.

Unlike Solomon, the generations after Abraham thrived, and his legacy of wealth carried on. Both of these men had a wonderful relationship with the Lord, and both were blessed. First Timothy 6:9-10 warns us, "But if it's only money these leaders are after, they'll self-destruct in no time. Lust for money brings trouble and nothing but trouble. Going down that path, some lose their footing in the faith completely and live to regret it bitterly ever after" (MSG). These verses describe the life of King Solomon as he eventually began to lust after wealth, which lead to destruction in the generations to come. Wealth did not destroy Solomon, but the lust for wealth and women did.

How to Handle Abundance Generously

With these examples, we can now start to examine ourselves and apply these historical records to our lives. Both of these men had an abundance of possessions. These possessions did not cause Abraham to fall. In relation to the questions I presented earlier about when enough is enough, it is clear that enough is enough when we can't control ourselves any longer, like King Solomon. It is when we forsake seeking the Lord for direction and hope and find these things in wealth. When we start to take our focus off the Lord, we have to fill our hearts with what it seeks.

These biographies start to paint a picture for how God calls us to manage abundance. Abundance does not always equate to millions and fancy cars. Many of you reading this book are considered wealthy by the world's standards. Many of us have resources beyond our needs.

Matthew 25:23 reminds us that *if* we can prove to be faithful with a "few things," then we will be put in charge of "many things." It is out of our abundance that the Lord calls us to give. First John 3:17 states, "If anyone has material possessions and sees his brother in need but has no pity on him, how can the love of God be in him?" If we see someone in need and the Lord prompts us to give, we are called to give. Does generosity always have to be a product of our abundance? No. When we look at the story of the poor widow, it is clear that she was not giving out of abundance; she "put in everything—all she had to live on" (Mark 12:44). Generosity is not solely a by-product of abundance but instead a condition of the heart. Therefore, there may be times when our hearts prompt us to be generous, yet our circumstances may not support our prompting. If our families are provided for and we feel a prompting from the Spirit to give, we may need to move outside of our own understanding. The widow certainly gave out of her own understanding. In this story, Jesus did not exclaim to his disciples, "Look at this foolish, poor widow. She just put in all she had to live on!" No, Jesus used her as an example, and he said to his disciples:

> "I tell you the truth, this poor widow has put more into the treasury than all the others. They all gave out of their wealth; but she, out of her poverty, put in everything—all she had to live on."
> Mark 12:43–44

The wealthy were throwing large amounts into the temple treasury, yet the widow only put in two small copper coins, worth only a few cents. While this was the case, Jesus said that she put in more than *all* the others. She did not put in more money, but rather faith. Generosity is the product of faith and obedience coming together: Faith + Obedience = Generosity.

The wealthy in this story gave because it was the law, and they gave a lot because they could. There is nothing wrong with this. Yet when we look at the widow, she gave from the last of her resources; she gave generously. Giving to honor your beliefs is one thing, but giving generously is quite another. Generosity is an inexplicable joy to support how the Lord is moving and jumping in to be a part of it!

Another example of extreme generosity rearing up in the hearts of believers can be found in 2 Corinthians 8:1–3.

> And now, brothers, we want you to know about the grace that God has given the Macedonian churches. Out of the most severe trial, their overflowing joy and their extreme poverty welled up in rich generosity. For I testify that they gave as much as they were able, and even beyond their ability.

These churches were motivated by their faith and obedience to the Lord, which lead to their generosity. In 2 Corinthians 8:2, the Greek word for generosity, *haplotes*, is defined as "formally 'the quality of singleness,' translated 'generosity,' the state of giving things in a manner that shows liberality; 'sincerity,' the moral quality of honesty expressing singleness of purpose or motivation."[4]

Do you remember how we were talking about motivation earlier? This verse and definition makes it clear that true generosity cannot be faked. It is 100 percent a condition of our hearts! In order to achieve generosity in our lives, we must first learn to exercise faith and obedience. A majority of the time, obedience is exercised in faith. Abraham obeyed God in regard to Isaac because he trusted that God knew best for him. It takes faith to obey. Obedience is not the natural response unless we trust and respect God. Romans 1:5 says, "Through him and for his name's sake, we received grace and apostleship to call people from among all the Gentiles to the obedience that comes from faith."

We are called to understand not only that abundance is a gift from God, but also that we are responsible to handle it generously! Some of you reading this book have abundance. Generosity is not always conditional. You are called to manage the resources entrusted to you in accordance with God's will. It is necessary that you first seek the heart of God through faith and obedience to Him. If you can do this, generosity will be the natural driver in all you do, thus bringing God glory!

Chapter 7:
What Is Tithing Today

In the last six chapters, we have grappled with questions on poverty and wealth. Now it's time to direct our attention back to chapter 1, which introduced the broken giving cycle. The truth is that your church is highly dependent on members' giving. The question then becomes "How can we get them to give more or give at all?" Your members' giving is critical to your church's financial health. This chapter is written in an effort to help you approach this need in a way that glorifies God and honors your members.

I often find myself perplexed when I hear pastors utilizing biblical text from the Old Testament to fuel giving in their churches, using text with commandments in conjunction with the Mosaic Law or preceding the Mosaic Law. While there are many principles that were carried into and under the New Covenant, I struggle to find how this is true in regard to a 10 percent tithe. My effort here is not to prove anyone wrong, but to challenge this thinking. It is my belief that God has so much more for your church and the Kingdom. Perhaps a 10 percent tithe limits all that God desires to do through your church and His people. Perhaps giving is no longer based on one's income but on the level of generosity residing in his or her heart. To start, let's take a step back and discuss the Old versus the New Covenant.

The Old versus New Covenant

Under the New Covenant we declare **freedom**. Galatians 5:1 states, "It is for freedom that Christ has set us free. Stand firm, then, and do not let yourselves be burdened again by a yoke of slavery."

The veil has been taken away between man and God (see 2 Cor. 3:16). This is the turning point. We are no longer bound by the Law. Jesus Christ has made us righteous before God through our belief in Him (see Rom. 10:4). This point is further demonstrated in Acts 15. In these verses, Paul and Barnabas confront the teaching that occurs as the Pharisees state, "Unless you are circumcised according to the custom taught by Moses, you cannot be saved" (Acts 15:1). Paul and Barnabas call this balderdash against the New Covenant. Peter, too, later rejects this belief among the Pharisees: "Now then, why do you try to test God by putting on the necks of the disciples a yoke that neither we nor our fathers have been able to bear? No! We believe it is through the grace of our Lord Jesus that we are saved, just as they are" (Acts 15:10–11). Paul, Barnabas, and now Peter challenge the Law of Moses, asserting that the grace imparted to us by Jesus Christ is greater. Peter describes the Law as a yoke that was unbearable not only for him, but also for the generations before him. The word *yoke* in Acts 15:10 and Galatians 5:1 translates back to the Greek word, *zygos,* which is defined as "to be in an oppressed condition such as slavery."[1] Today, many circulate the Law back into the New Covenant, the very thing Paul, Barnabas, and Peter were challenging so long ago. While the Law established valuable moral principles, these commandments are now trumped by the New Covenant.

> Therefore, there is now no condemnation for those who are in Christ Jesus, because through Christ Jesus the law of the Spirit of life set me free from the law of sin and death. For what the law was powerless to do in that it was weakened by the sinful nature, God did by sending his own Son in the likeness of sinful man to be a sin

offering. And so he condemned sin in sinful man, in order that the righteous requirements of the law might be fully met in us, who do not live according to sinful nature but according to the Spirit.
Romans 8:1–4

For sin shall not be your master, because you are not under the law, but under grace.
Romans 6:14

As noted in the definition of *zygos*, to be under a yoke means to be oppressed. Romans 8:1-4 further explains that the Law acted as a standard that lead to death verses life. You can imagine the high hurdles that the apostles faced as they presented the concept of grace to a belief system ruled by the Law for generations. The Pharisees clung to the slavery of the Law, while the hope of Jesus Christ was right before them; it was all they had ever known.

Before this faith came, we were held prisoners by the law, locked up until faith should be revealed.
Galatians 3:23

Today, it's important that the Law doesn't still hold us prisoner. We must remember that under the New Covenant, we are no longer under the Law; this includes a 10 percent tithe. We are capable of so much more! Under the New Covenant, we have moved from a robotic way of worship to one that directly accesses God. In this, the fruit that flows from our spirit becomes a powerful force (in Him). Giving is a critical piece in advancing the Kingdom. If it is undermined by limits, then the impact will suffer. So, what happens to tithing today?

Tithing Today

The principle of tithing 10 percent can be a trap. Let me gently elaborate on this. Many of us have been conditioned in the church to give 10 percent because the Bible says so. While it is what the Bible says, it is what the Bible says through God to Moses and to the Israelites. We are no longer under the rule of the Mosaic Law.

I have found that many Christians strive to give the church 10 percent, yet they don't know why, other than that's what they've been taught. This is sad because there is so much more! Under the New Covenant, we are called to give to God's missions with passion and excitement! **When we tithe just because someone told us to, we lose the beauty in the gift of giving.**

To be fair, in my own life and in the lives of others, I have seen true miracles happen in regard to tithing 10 percent. But that is not the whole story. In all cases, people were moving in faith (like the poor widow) and giving according to the principle of tithing. Yet ultimately what were they doing? Moving in faith! **This movement in faith defines what God looks for in us in relation to giving today.** God is not after you to give a particular percentage; He is after your heart and the hearts of those in your church.

So what's the message now? If it's not a 10 percent tithe, how do you teach about giving today? You do it through your church's mission. Money is vital in advancing your church's mission. Therefore, in order to function, your church needs funds. As we discussed in the giving cycle, your church depends primarily on its members to give. As you make this shift, your message moves from teaching your members to give more, just for the sake of routine giving; it moves to discipling them to give to the church's *mission*.

A mission is the reason why your church is in existence and what your church plans to do in the name of Jesus. While it is the mission of Christians to spread the gospel, there are many other missions that we can be a part of in an effort to advance the Kingdom.

The lack of giving in churches may be strongly correlated with the lack of mission in churches today. Perhaps this is why it feels like an uphill battle at times. After all, you're fulfilling the mission of the gospel, right? Yes, indeed, but that is only part of it. Perhaps the focus needs to shift from growing bigger to planning how we can utilize the church to advance His mission here on earth.

People give to things they believe in. Think about the number of emotionally charged commercials on TV showing abused animals, hungry children, and ravaged cities. These organizations know that by displaying their mission in the form of a commercial, they will receive the funds they need to keep fulfilling their mission. They make their mission real and visible to the audience. Most give to their church because they think they are supposed to, not always because they know and believe in the mission of their church. Of course this is not true for everyone, but I believe it is true for most. If churches work to clarify their mission, one that is specific and focused, I believe they can fulfill their mission! Perhaps by doing this, the struggle would become less.

If your church was to run a commercial now, what would you put in it—perhaps some images or a video of you on stage preaching, your congregation in worship, your children's ministry, or perhaps fun things that the teens did at camp this past summer? As an outsider who didn't know your church, would I understand your mission, other than being another church that I could attend?

In order to advance God's Kingdom, in order to ignite a passion for biblical stewardship within your church, you must stand as a mentor to those you serve. **You must present a clear, specific, and focused mission.** This mission is what people will be excited to be a part of and give to! Giving becomes a fulfillment of God's will, not an obligation.

Without the principle of tithing, most of us are left wondering where we should start. If we don't have 10 percent as a landmark, how much do we give? Even under the Old Covenant, God desired to see generosity in the hearts of His people. He actually commanded it. He also commands generosity from us today, and we can use this characteristic to be the barometer for our giving. The hard part about generosity is that it resides in our hearts and is an outflow of our love for the Father. As a pastor, it is very hard to force others into a closer relationship with Christ; they have to want it and make the change themselves. While this is the case, we can certainly train them up in the truths that God has given us in His Word in an effort to help them become the generous givers God created them to be!

Generosity

Generosity is not a product of financial well-being, but a stance of the heart. It is not a set percentage of one's income, but a desire to give toward something one believes in and supports. It is an expression of gratitude toward God. As Paul notes in 2 Corinthians 8:1-5, the Macedonian churches gave out of what they had, even beyond what they had, in order to "share in…service" of Paul's mission! Not only did they desire to give, they *pleaded*. In this same letter, Paul emphasizes the importance of giving generously in 2 Corinthians 9:6-8:

> Remember this: Whoever sows sparingly will also reap sparingly, and whoever sows generously will also reap generously. Each man should give what he has decided in his heart to give, not reluctantly

or under compulsion, for God loves a cheerful giver. And God is able to make all grace abound to you, so that in all things at all times, having all that you need, you will abound in every good work.

Giving should be done with a willing heart; we are called to "excel…in this grace of giving" (2 Cor. 8:7). Today, the generosity that Paul writes about is in danger of being stifled by the old: an empty, religious form of giving—the tithe. Generosity was clearly depicted in the lives of the Macedonians; they did not stop at 10 percent, but "they gave as much as they were able, and even beyond their ability" (2 Cor. 8:3). Giving today, under the New Covenant, is not about the 10 percent tithe, but about generosity. Generosity is the purest form of giving and what all believers in Christ are called to live out. This is the heart of Jesus. We are called to give to God and to those who live out the mission of God (see 2 Cor. 8). In an effort to understand what true generosity looks like, let's deconstruct 2 Corinthians 9:6–15:

> Remember this: Whoever sows sparingly will also reap sparingly, and whoever sows generously will also reap generously. Each man should give what he has decided in his heart to give, not reluctantly or under compulsion, for God loves a cheerful giver. And God is able to make all grace abound to you, so that in all things at all times, having all that you need, you will abound in every good work. As it is written:
>> "He has scattered abroad his gifts to the poor; his righteousness endures forever."
>
> Now he who supplies seed to the sower and bread for food will also supply and increase your store of seed and will enlarge the harvest

of your righteousness. You will be made rich in every way so that you can be generous on every occasion, and through us your generosity will result in thanksgiving to God. This service that you perform is not only supplying the needs of God's people but is also overflowing in many expressions of thanks to God. Because of the service by which you have proved yourselves, men will praise God for the obedience that accompanies your confession of the gospel of Christ, and for your generosity in sharing with them and with everyone else. And in their prayers for you their hearts will go out to you, because of the surpassing grace God has given you. Thanks be to God for his indescribable gift!

I am so grateful for the juxtaposition presented in these words. These verses embody the heart of God under the New Covenant. They also reveal the heart of God before the New Covenant. These principles were present under the Mosaic Law in regard to helping and giving to the poor and fellow brothers. We are still called to give, but the beauty of it is so much greater because the motive is not fueled by the Law, but instead by love and the grace of God.

Verse 6:
Remember this: Whoever sows sparingly will also reap sparingly, and whoever sows generously will also reap generously.

What we put into anything is what we will get out of it. This is the beautiful universal truth that God has put into order over everything. Here, we are urged to undertake this principle in regard to our giving.

Verse 7:

Each man should give what he has decided in his heart to give, not reluctantly or under compulsion, for God loves a cheerful giver.

In addition to understanding the principle of reaping what we sow, Paul further expands upon the fact that while this is the case, what we give should not be solely for what we can get back, but rather fueled by the willingness to give from our hearts.

Verse 8:

And God is able to make all grace abound to you, so that in all things at all times, having all that you need, you will abound in every good work.

Just as Paul correlates grace with giving in this verse, he also does so to show the key that fueled the Macedonian's excitement to give. It was the grace of God that prompted them to give all that they had and more. Here, Paul's plea for us is that we, too, are subject to this grace so that we might give generously, recognizing that our willingness can only be enhanced by grace.

Verses 9–12:

As it is written: "He has scattered abroad his gifts to the poor; his righteousness endures forever." Now he who supplies seed to the sower and bread for food will also supply and increase your store of seed and will enlarge the harvest of your righteousness. You will be made rich in every way so that you can be generous on every occasion, and through us your generosity will result in thanksgiving to God. This service that you perform is not only supplying the needs of God's people but is also overflowing in many expressions of thanks to God.

The meaning of our partnership with God in giving deepens. We move to supply the needs of others through the resources that God has entrusted to us, thus bringing Him glory. It's not about us. It's about Him and directing others toward His goodness.

Verses 13–15:
Because of the service by which you have proved yourselves, men will praise God for the obedience that accompanies your confession of the gospel of Christ, and for your generosity in sharing with them and with everyone else. And in their prayers for you their hearts will go out to you, because of the surpassing grace God has given you. Thanks be to God for his indescribable gift!

Generosity becomes an expression of faith that directs others toward the Father, thus amplifying the gospel of Christ. Generosity becomes a great expression of faith and serves to be a *key ingredient* to helping change the hearts of people.

The spark that we can now create for the gospel in the hearts of the lost comes through our generosity. Not only does this generosity work to support the mission of God, but also to touch the lives of those around us. In James 2:14–19, we are reminded that faith without works is dead. In addition to this clear warning, notice how James highlights those in need:

What good is it, my brothers, if a man claims to have faith but has no deeds? Can such faith save him? Suppose a brother or sister is without clothes and daily food. If one of you says to him, "Go, I wish you well; keep warm and well fed," but does nothing about his physical needs, what good is it? In the same way, faith by itself, if it is not accompanied by action is dead. But someone will say, "You have faith; I have deeds." Show me your faith without deeds, and I will show you my faith by what I do. You believe that there is one God. Good! Even the demons believe that—and shudder."

Though many may believe that there is a God, or a *higher power*, even the demons believe that! For unbelievers in need, who may or may not believe in God, their belief can become further solidified through our generosity!

Giving today goes beyond tithing 10 percent. We are not fulfilling a law in order to remain in good standing with God. Today we give generously because we desire to see the needs of others met, and by our actions, direct them to Jesus. As a church, teach your members about generosity and clarify your mission. Encourage members to join your mission. If they don't align with it, then they may leave. This is the risk you take, but what is it about—numbers or impact?

Today we make it about the numbers. Why not make it about mission? Once we're able to clearly define our mission, it will be natural that others join around what we're doing. It will be natural for them to want to support the efforts we're making toward advancing the Kingdom!

When we start to grasp the freedom in the New Covenant, it is *new* life. The pieces of the Old and New Covenant come together under the expression by which we are called to live. The gospel of Christ is tied to our hearts, from which generosity flows. Directing the glory to Him and advancing His mission—that is what it's all about!

What's Next?

The last seven chapters have poured the foundation for your next step: doing. You move from pupil to intern. It is now time to take what we've studied and apply it to your personal finances. The next four chapters will teach you how to become a better financial steward over your household in order to help you answer to the question that Paul posed to church leaders in 1 Timothy 3:5:

> If anyone does not know how to manage his own family, how can he take care of God's church?

You must first gain a handle over your household finances in order to confidently lead in finances at your church. This process may prove to be uncomfortable and painful for some, yet it is critical.

We started with reflecting inward through the Money Quiz. Now we move to implementing what we're learning so that we can live it out and be the example that we're called to be. As you are moving through this process, remember it's not about getting it perfect. The ultimate goal is a heart change.

As you move from the foundation of the *why* to the *how*, utilize *The Stewardship Movement Video Series and Study Guide* to not only help train you up, but also your leadership.

My goal is to do the teaching for you and to make it a fun experience. You are well on your way to a better relationship with money—keep it up!

Part II: Live

Chapter 8:
Financial Management

Over the course of the last seven chapters, we have discovered the *why*: why we're called to handle our finances in a way that glorifies God. This is so critical because our relationship with money is one that we will have for the rest of our lives. The sooner we can get this, the better. While we have explored the heart of the *why*, now it's time to jump into the practical side of the *how*: how to manage our finances in a way that brings glory to our Father and advances His Kingdom. Finances are a critical area we will have to account for to God. We will take the truths we have learned and now apply them on a practical level. Yet I warn you: until a heart shift takes place in regard to the principles you have learned thus far, you are still bound by your old patterns. In other words, if your heart is still in the same place about how you view money and think God views it, then this guidance won't stick.

If you are ready to go deeper with yourself, with your leadership, and with your church, then now is the time to get access to *The Stewardship Movement Video Series and Study Guide* (if you haven't already) while you are making your way through these next chapters. This video series and guide go into depth about all the principles we have discussed so far, plus how to manage a budget, pay down debt, save more, and gain a solid understanding of your finances. You can also gain access to tools that will help you manage all of these important tasks in an easy and fun way! To access the videos and guide, go to www.TheStewardshipMovement.com.

I am confident that there is freedom for you in regard to your per-

-sonal finances, your church's finances, and the finances of those who attend your church. As we start to journey down this path, some of you may be combating sweaty palms. I want to reassure you that there is nothing to fear. Over the years, I have found that many people are ashamed of what their finances look like. Remember, it is not what we look like on the outside that the Lord is concerned with, but rather our hearts.

> "The Lord does not look at the things man looks at. Man looks at the outward appearance, but the Lord looks at the heart."
> 1 Samuel 16:7

The priority is getting our hearts in the right place about money. While the rest can look like shambles to man, God is after the heart. Remember to start there. Once you have addressed your heart, you can start to pick up the rubble.

Not only can shame prevent us from confronting our financial circumstances, but also so can our fears. For so long I avoided numbers and finances because I told myself that I was horrible with numbers. So if you were like me, stop speaking curses over yourself. God can extract greatness out of each of us if we're willing. If you are willing to face your finances head on, I believe God will bless you for that. I speak from personal experience and with many *case studies*. Over the years that I counseled clients, I saw God continually bless them for their willingness to get their finances in order. This is why I say that it is critical that your heart be ready for this—locked and loaded, ready to press forward. God blessed those who remained steadfast in this pursuit. I cannot guarantee this for you, but I can attest to what I saw in the lives of those who fervently sought God in this area. The motions that they were going through with me were to bring God glory, not to look good to me. Never fear your incapability because in Christ all things are possible. I had a client who thought I was crazy when I told her that she would be the one to calculate the budget every week and manage the Microsoft Excel spread sheet. I will never forget when I got a message from her about five months after we started; she was jumping up and down—she finally *got it*. She eventually came to love the process that she at first dreaded, doubting her ability to do it. This happened because she embraced the process. In this process, she and her husband embraced the heart of their Father, not the budget. Do you see the difference here? This really isn't even about the budget. It's about loving the Lord your God with all your heart, mind, and strength and digging deep to honor Him. As you begin this process, remember that change will not happen overnight, but if you keep at it, you will see results.

In these chapters we will review how you first need to manage your finances for you and your family, not your church. Until you get your household in order, you certainly can't help to get your church in order.

> Here is a trustworthy saying: If anyone sets his heart on being an overseer, he desires a noble task. Now the overseer must be above reproach, the husband of but one wife, temperate, self-controlled, respectable, hospitable, able to teach, not given to drunkenness, not violent but gentle, not quarrelsome, not a lover of money. He must manage his own family well and see that his children obey him with proper respect. (If anyone does not know how to manage his own family, how can he take care of God's church?)
> 1 Timothy 3:1–5

Regardless of your financial circumstances, you can succeed financially. Bankruptcy? Credit-card debt? Medical bills? High interest rates? Looming student loans? IRS taxes? No savings? Kids in college? Refrigerator breakdown? All of these things are what's called *life*, and we *all* experience them.

> [You] know that your brothers throughout the world are undergoing the same kind of sufferings.
> 1 Peter 5:9

Your circumstances are no different than the majority of the people surrounding you. The moment we start to allow our circumstances to define us, we die—maybe not literally, but in heart. It can be sinful to resort to giving up when we have the Holy Spirit living inside of us! So how do we tackle all of the circumstances we encounter? How do we gain a little bit of ground so that when tough times come, we're prepared? The first step is to get organized. Get your finances organized by creating a budget. Before you throw me over the edge, hear me out. While most of us equate budgets with restriction, they actually equate to freedom. Let's illustrate this point. A mentor offered this illustration to me once, and I feel like it paints a great picture:

> You just purchased a home off a busy street. Six lanes of traffic zoom up and down the backside of your backyard all day long. Your backyard is huge with a beautiful view of the mountains. It is like your own park right in your own backyard. While this space is lovely, you are nervous about your children playing outside due to this busy road. One of your first home projects is to build a fence so that your view of traffic is blocked, but also so that your children

can safely go outside and play. The moment that the last fence slat is installed, the freedom for your family is greatly increased! Now you can send your children outside to play and not fear the traffic.

In this illustration, your budget is the fence. While some could consider a fence restrictive, in this case it provides great freedom. By building the fence, you have a better awareness of your yard's perimeter, which brings comfort to know that your children are now safe.

Because most of us don't have budgets, we are essentially blind to our financial state. We operate in a survival and strife mode due to ignorance. This is not freedom. Christ came to set us free from all things and finances are not immune to this. Since a budget brings awareness to our current financial state, many of us avoid doing one. If we can just get past this hump of insecurity, we may find that this thing we fear so much might actually bring great freedom. Most of us don't want to face money in our lives because of our past experiences with it. We avoid talking about money and having to deal with it. Without a change, we may be bound in this area for the rest of our lives. Because a majority of us avoid money, it really wreaks havoc in our homes. **It is time to face our finances with courage and to no longer allow shame or fear to hold us back.** It is time to get focused on what is ahead instead of looking back to our financial regrets. Proverbs 4:25–27 states:

> Let your eyes look straight ahead,
> fix your gaze directly before you.
> Make level paths for your feet,
> and take only ways that are firm.
> Do not swerve to the right or to the left;
> keep your foot from evil.

Because our financial circumstances do not define who we are, we cannot allow the glitches to get us off track. We can start to build structures so that we can experience freedom in all circumstances, positive or negative. It is important that we become the manager over the resources we've been entrusted with so that they don't have the opportunity to manage us. In order to become a manager over your finances, you need to put up a fence through tools like a budget, savings plan, and debt-reduction plan—and no more telling ourselves that we are bad with numbers. If we keep speaking that lie over ourselves, then it will continue to permeate our hearts. We start today by speaking truth over ourselves. Instead of telling yourself that you're bad with numbers, say "I can do this!" Let's make Galatians 5:1 our motto moving forward: "Christ has set us free to live a free life. So take your stand! Never again let anyone put a harness of slavery on you" (MSG).

In this newfound freedom, it is now time to *plunge* into the first step. Take a moment to answer the following three questions:

1. What was your net income last month?
2. What were your total expenses?
3. What was your cash flow?

When people answer these questions, they usually fall into one of three categories:

1. They don't know the numbers and don't have them written down anywhere.

2. They kind of know these numbers but don't have them written down anywhere.

3. They concretely know these numbers and have them written down somewhere.

The truth is that until we concretely know these numbers each month, we will never be able to prepare for future circumstances. This principle is not just applicable to our finances, but it is also applicable to life. We will reap what we sow in *all* areas of our lives. With this said, we need to get our finances organized and in order. This process takes time, and it does not happen overnight. Give yourself six to twelve months to get comfortable and to find a rhythm.

Start by writing down your net monthly income and expenses. Then, calculate your cash flow by subtracting your expenses from your income.

Be sure to complete this step before moving on to the next chapter, you will need it moving forward.

Chapter 9:
Setting Goals and Budgeting

Financial management and accountability are the beginning of freedom. As with anything in life, until we face reality, we will continue in our old ways, never to know what's on the other side of change. In the last chapter, we started to make the shift from the *why* to the *how*. How do we now apply this knowledge to our lives? How do we handle our finances in a way that glorifies God? To some of us, thinking of money and managing it in a way that glorifies God are foreign subjects, which I hope now have come to life.

This chapter is the beginning of the **how** for you. The rest of the chapters that follow will usher you into implementing these practices in your finances, thus fulfilling the goal of honoring God with them. By reviewing these important steps and also through implementing the tools provided, you will start to *live out* stewardship in your own life. So, where to start?

We start with goals and then move to your budget. Goals can be a tricky subject for believers because our hearts' cry is to listen to the Father. Sometimes it feels that by setting goals, without proper acknowledgment of God's will, we may miss the mark. Perhaps we can view goals differently in regard to our finances. I do believe that there is a healthy way to combine what we have learned about God's heart for money and how, by setting goals, we can create a stable financial future for our family and also give to others generously. While I am not there to sit with you and weigh your goals against what we know about God's heart and money, I do encourage you to weigh your goals against what we've studied thus far.

Goals

If you have ever done a home project, you know that it takes planning and preparation. If you have ever built a house, you really know the level of planning, goal setting, preparation, and commitment it takes. Building a budget toward financial freedom requires the same steps. We set goals, make plans, adjust plans as unexpected expenses arise, and stay committed to the big picture. As we set goals in relation to our finances, it is critical to remember that goals are the framework. Just as with any home-improvement project, you will run into unexpected circumstances. You can plan until you are blue in the face, yet the likelihood of running into the unforeseen is very likely. The same goes for planning in relation to doing it with God. I am a big planner, yet over the years God has slowly shown me that while my plans may be good, they are not always in His will or timing. This lesson goes back to holding things loosely. We all need to plan because if we don't, then we're floundering.

While this is true, we must also pause first to ask God what His plans are. Sometimes, God's voice may not be as clear to some of us as it seems to be to others. If His voice does not seem clear to you, get into a quiet place with no distractions—no noise, no kids, no pets, no spouse, and no friends—a room in your house that brings you peace or a rock of solitude in the woods, and then just close your eyes and listen. I do feel that when we still our spirit before God, He speaks. Even if it's not words, He can still move in our spirit. Right now as I write this, I am in my office. It is snowing outside, and I have the window cracked (and the heat on, too—ha). The snow is refracting its glow into the room, and the wind is blowing across the trees every fifteen seconds or so. It is beautiful, and I feel surrounded by the Father. It doesn't have to be complicated. Seek His will first, always. Sometimes His voice may be a rest or unrest in your spirit. Ultimately seek His will before yours. He wants the best for us. I know the times that I haven't listened and went my own way, I wasted a bunch of time and missed out on the blessings of God. The most beautiful part of this whole picture is that even though we may make mistakes in this, God's blessing can still fall on us.

As we seek God's will in relation to our financial goals, it is critical that we hold these goals loosely. This doesn't mean don't work as hard toward your financial goals, but to just be open first and foremost to the Father if He asks you to do something else.

> Now listen, you who say, "Today or tomorrow we will go to this or that city, spend a year there, carry on business and make money." Why, you do not even know what will happen tomorrow. What is your life? You are a mist that appears for a little while and then vanishes. Instead, you ought to say, "If it is the Lord's will, we will live and do this or that." As it is, you boast and brag. All such boasting is evil.
> James 4:13–16

The *Asbury Bible Commentary* suggests that goal setting in itself is not evil in conjunction with these verses. However, ignoring God and boasting about what you are going to do tomorrow, when you don't ultimately hold the power to make it happen, is:

> Accumulating goods may not always engender strife, but it may precipitate another sinful attitude that is counter to the spirit of

Jesus, hyper-self-confidence with a total disregard of God. Phillips translates 4:16: "You take a certain pride in planning with such confidence." James paints a picture of businessmen who are programming their business activities for the next year. When they say, "We will go to this or that city," they use the indicative mood of the verb. The nuance is that of an undaunted determination that will not possibly be thwarted. They are in full control of the future as they plot their destination and profits. Their fault, however, is that they are forgetful of the frailty of life. The opening word of the Greek text of v. 14 ("Why"), which is generally not expressed by translators, suggests that James is insinuating, "Who do you think you are?" He likens their life to visible smoke or water vapor, which can disappear suddenly by a change in wind or temperature. These traders not only disregard God, they also flaunt his will. This kind of arrogance is not only disgusting; it is sinful, too.[1]

Bottom line: goal setting needs to be submissive to the will of the Father. We do need plans to build a house or improve it, yet we are bound to have to modify plans because of things that we didn't plan for. With this groundwork set, creating goals and plans in our finances can help us achieve God-directed goals.

Goal setting is liberating and powerful. It affords us the opportunity to see things that we hope for on paper, which in essence makes them feel more attainable. I know that when I am running around in a flurry, Stephen can tell that I am overwhelmed, and he often asks me, "Have you written your thoughts down?" It is a good reminder that if I can see my thoughts on paper, I am more likely to wrap my head around what needs to be accomplished. The same goes with your financial goals. Credit-card debt, mortgage rates, college tuition, student loans, bills, lack of savings, and deteriorating cars are all overwhelming. Keeping this stress all bottled up inside is not healthy! You need to get it down on paper. Do it now.

Start by writing down your financial goals on paper. If you are married, this will involve communicating with your spouse. I would like each of you to identify three individual goals, and in addition to these, three common goals. If you are married, that is a total of nine different goals. If you are single, it is a total of three. These goals should be something that you want to achieve in the next twelve months. Over the years I have found that women would typically put down common goals for their individual goals. Some examples are pay off debt, get John braces, get a car for Mike, and so on. There is nothing wrong with these goals, but I want the ladies (or, gentlemen, if you find yourselves doing this, too) to shift their focus for this exercise. For this exercise, count these types of goals toward the common goal list. Your individual goals should consist of things that you personally would like to work toward. Guys, maybe it's a new tool or grill. For the ladies, perhaps it's a new home decor item or a piece of furniture. Whatever these may be, they are things you like and would bring you pleasure (and something that your spouse would probably care less about).

Once your three individual goals are written down, come together and tackle your three common goals. At the end of this process, here is what you'll want on paper:

Individual Goals—single/married
In the next twelve months, I would like to accomplish the following (three) financial goals (each spouse – if married, a total of six goals, three each).

Joint Goals—married

In the next twelve months, we would like to accomplish the following (three) financial goals (combined financial goals, different from individual goals).

Once these goals are written down, you're ready to move to budgeting. Are you surprised that goals come before budgets? There can't be a plan for money (budget) without knowing where you want to go (goals).

Budget

From the small exercise at the end of the last chapter, you should have your net monthly income and expenses written down. Now it is time to determine how we can utilize a budget for your household to help keep you on track financially, which will ultimately bring freedom. **The budget is a powerful tool that will enable you to accomplish the financial goals that you have written down.**

Now we'll take your financial goals for the next twelve months and fit them into your budget. **Your budget is the ticket to accomplishing your financial goals**—the blueprint for your financial redesign. It will provide the structure you need, and if you are consistent, you will see your goals come to fruition.

In an ideal situation, I'd be sitting with you at your kitchen table, pondering numbers. I love it when the numbers come alive! While I cannot personally sit down with you, I am going to walk you through the process in the following pages, just as if I were sitting with you at your table. Remember that your budget is designed to help you, but it takes time to become comfortable with its guidance. Give yourself at least six to twelve months to adjust to having one. While I have met those of you who will get your budget 99.9 percent spot on each month, don't beat yourself up if you are not one of these individuals. I encourage you all to work toward staying within the boundaries of the budget, but don't hold yourself or your spouse to a standard of perfection.

Before we begin, an important first step to building a budget is to understand all the pieces that make it up. On the next page is a picture of the MAP Budget Tool. We will utilize this tool to study the different parts of the budget, and so as we are discussing them, you will have a point of reference. In an effort to honor those who may not be able to utilize the MAP Budget Tool at this time, I will be teaching you how to build your budget manually in the following section. If you are interested in accessing the MAP Budget Tool, which will help automate the process of budgeting for you, you can do so at www.TheStewardshipMovement.com.

What Makes Up a Budget?

A budget is made up of very basic data. First and foremost, your budget is made up of your income and expenses. Your expenses also include your debt payments and savings transfers. In order to properly account for these items, we need to utilize the following measures:

Actual Amount: the amount received or spent to date for the specific income or expense.

Budgeted Amount: the projected or set amount for income and expenses.

Remainder: the amount remaining for a specific income or expense item.

Cash Flow: the amount left over at the end of the month; income minus expenses (including debt and savings transfers).

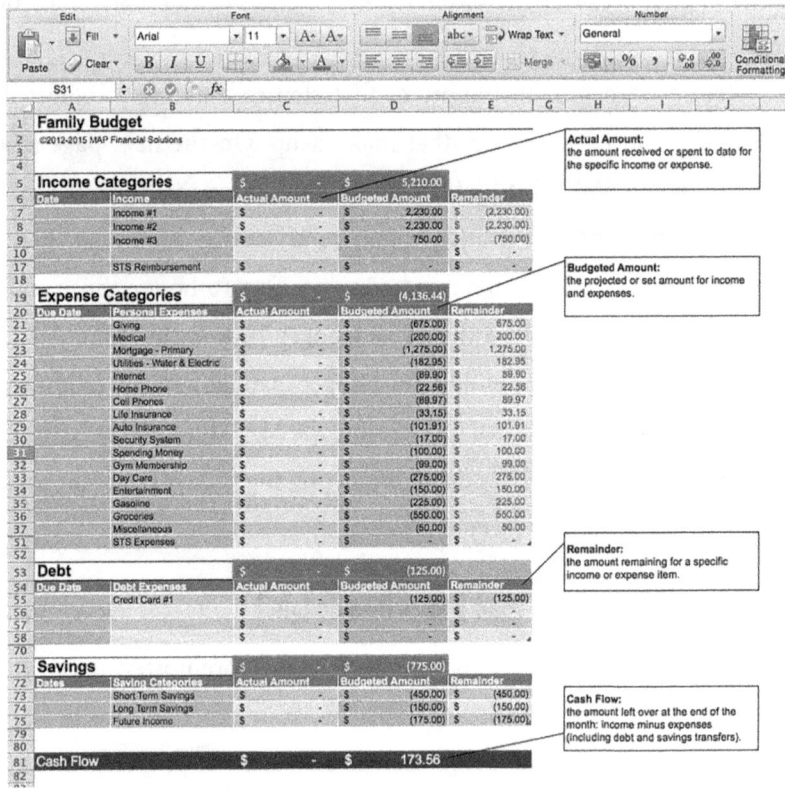

Image captured from Microsoft Excel.

Part I: Create Your Budget

Now, you will utilize a list of steps to create your budget. Again, it's a manual process, so take out a ruled notebook and follow along. Even if you purchased the MAP Budget Tool, this work won't be in vain.

Step One

The first step is to identify all sources of your monthly income. I recommend that you simply write down your net income. Your net income is the income that you *take* home after taxes and other deductions.

Think of it as pulling up fish onto a boat with a net. The fish that you pull up and onto your boat (with the net) is your *net* - what you'll bring home. The *gross* represents the total number of fish in your net before you brought it up (some of the fish are lost through the net in the process of pulling it up to the boat).

Your gross income is reduced to your net because of things taken out of your gross income like health insurance, taxes, social security, retirement-account contributions, and so forth. While some recommend utilizing gross income when creating a budget, I've found it easier for clients to utilize net. Again, the goal is not to turn you into an analytical math whiz, but to broaden your understanding of where your money is going. If you're doing this process manually, I recommend that you start your budget in a blank, ruled notebook. On the first page, you are going to write down the first draft of your budget. For illustration purposes we will be referring to Tom and Lisa's budget.

First, at the top of the page, make a header that says *Budget*. Then, write down your net monthly income in the format shown below and total it up. Be sure to leave space for two additional columns to the left and to the right of your *Budgeted* column that we'll be adding later.

BUDGET

Income	Budgeted
Tom Paycheck #1	$1750
Tom Paycheck #2	$1750
Total Income	**$3500**

Step Two

Next, below your income, write down your expenses in the format shown and then total them up.

BUDGET

Income	Budgeted
Tom Paycheck #1	$1750
Tom Paycheck #2	$1750
Total Income	**$3500**

Expenses	Budgeted
Giving	($350)
Mortgage—Primary	($1125)
Utilities—Electrical, Water	($175)
Internet and Home Phone	($87)
Cell Phones	($81)
Insurance—Auto	($99.25)
Insurance—Life	($22.50)
Spending Money	($100)
Entertainment	($100)
Groceries	($600)
Gasoline	($200)
Savings	($50)
Credit Card	($20)
Student Loan	($79)
Car Loan #1	($225)
Car Loan #2	($180)
Personal Care	($60)
Miscellaneous	($25)
Total Expenses	**($3578.75)**

Following are a few important notes about the *expenses*.

First, notice the parentheses around the amounts. While I don't expect you all to be math whizzes, I do want you to understand the basic *flow* of money. Money *in* is **positive**. Money *out* is **negative**. The parentheses indicate money going out. Whenever you are inputting or writing down expenses, get in the habit of putting the number in parentheses.

Second, notice how I didn't just round everything. When writing down your expenses, don't just guess or round the totals. Go to your statements and write down the exact amounts. For expenses like groceries and gas, your budgeted number will be rounded because these items don't have a bill amount associated with them.

Third, this is a very basic expense list that does not include all of the expense categories I have seen over the years, so don't stop here. This is just an example, so be sure to evaluate all of your expenses for the month and just use this as a guide.

Step Three

Calculate your monthly cash flow. Your monthly cash flow is calculated by subtracting your expenses from your income. For this example, the calculation would look like this:

Monthly Income - Monthly Expenses = Monthly Cash Flow
$3500   ($3578.75)   ($78.75)

As you can see, Tom and Lisa are driving a negative monthly cash flow. When people first construct their budget, a lot of them see a negative cash flow. We will address how to correct this later in the chapter. For now, I just want you to get these numbers down.

Step Four

Flip to a new piece of a paper in your notebook, a few pages after your budget. At the top of this page, make a header that says *Budget Tracking*.

This sheet is to simply track your expenses on a weekly basis; after all, what is the point of a budget if you're not tracking your expenses each week to ensure that you are not going over budget?

On this sheet, you'll list the date that you spent money, where you spent money, how much money you spent, and what category on your budget this amount should be assigned to. Record this information in the format shown below:

BUDGET TRACKING

Date	Place	Amount	Category
8/1	Tom Paycheck #1	$1750	Income
8/9	Vitamin Store	($89.19)	Groceries
8/9	Grocery Store	($125.14)	Groceries
8/15	Café	($28.19)	Entertainment
8/17	Cleaners	($12.58)	Miscellaneous

On a weekly basis, you will tabulate these totals and ensure that you are not going over your budgeted amounts. You will have some expenses that will always be the same, such as your mortgage or insurance. For expenses like gas, groceries, and entertainment, you will have to measure them against your budget. For instance, the grocery budget for Tom and Lisa is $600 per month. So far, they have spent $214.33 as depicted in the tracking above. This means that they have $385.67 left for groceries.

Step Five

Now that you have your budget created on the first page and your tracking sheet started, it is time to flip back to your Budget sheet. We are going to add one column to the left and one to the right of your *Budgeted* column.

On your Budget sheet, add a column to the left of the *Budgeted* column with the heading *Actual*. Then, to the right of the *Budgeted* column, add a column with the heading *Remainder*. Then, log any actual expenses for the month so far under the *Actual* column from your Tracking Sheet.

You will be updating these columns on a weekly basis according to your Tracking Sheet, so you will need to use pencil for these. Each week, under the *Actual* column, you are going to record when income and expenses are realized. For expenses that accrue over the month like gas and groceries, you will need to add these and update the amounts. The *Remainder* column is then the difference between what you budgeted for and what you have actually spent.

Create these columns in the format as shown.

BUDGET

Income	Actual	Budgeted	Remainder
Tom Paycheck #1	$1750	$1750	$0
Tom Paycheck #2	$0	$1750	$1750
Total Income	**$1750**	**$3500**	**$1750**

Expenses	Actual	Budgeted	Remainder
Giving	($0)	($350)	$350
Mortgage—Primary	($0)	($1125)	$1125
Utilities—Electrical, Water	($0)	($175)	$175
Internet and Home Phone	($0)	($87)	$87
Cell Phones	($0)	($81)	$81

Expenses	Actual	Budgeted	Remainder
Insurance—Auto	($0)	($99.25)	$99.25
Insurance—Life	($0)	($22.50)	$22.50
Spending Money	($0)	($100)	$100
Entertainment	($28.19)	($100)	$71.81
Groceries	($214.33)	($600)	$385.67
Gasoline	($0)	($200)	$200
Savings	($0)	($50)	$50
Credit Card	($0)	($20)	$20
Student Loan	($0)	($79)	$79
Car Loan #1	($0)	($225)	$225
Car Loan #2	($0)	($180)	$180
Personal Care	($0)	($60)	$60
Miscellaneous	($12.58)	($25)	$12.42
Total Expenses	**($255.10)**	**($3578.75)**	**$3323.65**

This is how you can budget manually; I don't want anyone to miss the opportunity to learn how to budget if they don't have access to Microsoft Excel. Yet, in an effort to save you time, I would strongly urge you to work toward getting the MAP Budget Tool. It will save you time—budget for it!

Part II: Create a Positive Cash Flow

Now that we have created the skeleton for Tom and Lisa's budget, it is time that we address their cash-flow issue—a negative cash flow. Just like them, when you run your budget, you may find that your monthly net income minus expenses is a negative number. If this is the case, know that you're not alone. When I first met with clients, many would find themselves anywhere from a ($100) to ($500) cash flow monthly.

They could not understand how this was happening because they were not feeling the pinch. But you can't spend negative money. Either savings or credit cards were supplementing the difference. We will talk about how to correct this soon but before we do, let's keep moving down the path for creating a positive cash flow together (this includes those of you who are not driving a negative cash flow each month).

Some financial counselors will counsel that you *zero* out your budget (which is not a bad plan), but I am going to suggest you do something differently to create a padding for yourself, a cushion. A cushion is a safety net that you build up for yourself. Think of it like overdraft protection. It is money left over after expenses. You don't spend it, but it gives you the comfort of knowing that you have more than zero in the end, as one of my clients called it, "The new zero!" Yes, indeed, it is your new zero! Your cushion amount is up to you. It depends on how much you have left over and what feels comfortable. Typical cushion amounts are $100, $250, $300, or $500. This means that instead of your income minus expenses equaling zero, they will equal your cushion. Be sure to continue any overdraft protection that you have on your accounts—this is just a good measure.

In regard to Tom and Lisa's budget (and yours, too, if you are driving a negative cash flow each month), in order to create a positive cash flow, we will need to first cut expenses. As we're cutting expenses we will also work to create a positive cushion for them. A cushion is an amount that will be built up over time according to your budget. Once you reach your goal cushion amount and it's in your bank account, you can then zero out your budget if you would like.

As you're looking through Tom and Lisa's budget, be reflecting on your own budget. Highlight the items that may be considered *nonessentials*. These might include items like entertainment or spending money. You may not have to eliminate these entirely, just reduce the amount you allocate towards them each month. On Tom and Lisa's budget, I have put a star to the left of the items that need to be reduced in order to create a positive cash flow:

Tom and Lisa's Revised Budget
BUDGET

Income	Actual	Budgeted	Remainder
Tom Paycheck #1	$1750	$1750	$0
Tom Paycheck #2	$0	$1750	$1750
Total Income	**$1750**	**$3500**	**$1750**

Expenses	Actual	Budgeted	Remainder
Giving	($0)	($350)	$350
Mortgage—Primary	($0)	($1125)	$1125
Utilities—Electrical, Water	($0)	($175)	$175
Internet and Home Phone	($0)	($87)	$87
Cell Phones	($0)	($81)	$81
Insurance—Auto	($0)	($99.25)	$99.25
Insurance—Life	($0)	($22.50)	$22.50
*Spending Money	($0)	($0)	$0
*Entertainment	($28.19)	($50)	$21.81
Groceries	($214.33)	($600)	$385.67
Gasoline	($0)	($200)	$200
Savings	($0)	($50)	$50
Credit Card	($0)	($20)	$20
Student Loan	($0)	($79)	$79
Car Loan #1	($0)	($225)	$225
Car Loan #2	($0)	($180)	$180

Expenses	Actual	Budgeted	Remainder
Personal Care	($0)	($60)	$60
Miscellaneous	($12.58)	($25)	$12.42
Total Expenses	**($255.10)**	**($3428.75)**	**$3173.65**

Tom and Lisa's Revised Cash Flow

Monthly Income	-	Monthly Expenses	=	Monthly Cash Flow
$3500		($3428.75)		$71.25

While we have achieved a positive cash flow for Tom and Lisa, they are not paying down their debt any faster. Saving and paying down debt is dependent on one thing—income. If your income only covers your essential expenses and minimum payments on your credit cards and loans, the rate of your debt-reduction and savings will be much slower.

In order to further solidify the practice of freeing up cash, let's talk about two real examples of clients' budgets (their names have been changed to protect their identities). The first client, Melissa, was driving a negative cash flow each month. The second clients, Mike and Sarah, had an abundance of cash at the end of the month, but they didn't know where it was going? Let's review these budgets now.

Melissa

When Melissa and I sat down to review her budget, it reflected a cash flow of ($2) each month. When we got into discussion, ($2) was actually around ($200)! This was because she was not tracking all of her expenses like skiing trips, concerts, and other impromptu purchases. The few-hundred-dollar deficit was ending up on her credit card each month. In turn, her credit card was accumulating a balance and was being paid at the minimum amount due.

Melissa had three goals: pay off her student loan, pay off her credit card debt, and to increase her income. In reviewing her budget, we determined that in order to create a positive cash flow, we would have to reduce some of her expenses. In addition to this, we discussed that if she wanted to pay off debt at the rate she desired, she would need to increase income. Telling clients that their only solution to achieving their goals is to increase their income can be really hard news to deliver, especially if they are working full time and have no extra time. The thought of taking on something else for a source of income is daunting. Melissa's advantage was that she was self-employed and was able to increase her income to around $3,000 per month (from $1,200 when we first met).

A	B	C	D	E
Budget - Melissa				
©2012-2015 MAP Financial Solutions				
Income Categories		$ -	$ 1,200.00	
Date	Income	Actual Amount	Budgeted Amount	Remainder
	Income #1	$ -	$ 1,200.00	$ (1,200.00)
	Income #2	$ -	$ -	$ -
	Other	$ -	$ -	$ -
	STS Reimbursement	$ -	$ -	$ -
Expense Categories		$ -	$ (1,055.00)	
Due Date	Personal Expenses	Actual Amount	Budgeted Amount	Remainder
	Charity	$ -	$ -	$ -
	Rent	$ -	$ (470.00)	$ 470.00
	Utilities - Water & Electric	$ -	$ (28.00)	$ 28.00
	Cable	$ -	$ (24.00)	$ 24.00
	Personal Care	$ -	$ -	$ -
	Cell Phone	$ -	$ (74.00)	$ 74.00
	Life Insurance	$ -	$ (27.00)	$ 27.00
	Auto Insurance	$ -	$ (86.00)	$ 86.00
	Renters Insurance	$ -	$ (18.00)	$ 18.00
	Entertainment	$ -	$ -	$ -
	Eating Out	$ -	$ -	$ -
	Gasoline	$ -	$ (160.00)	$ 160.00
	Groceries	$ -	$ (150.00)	$ 150.00
	Miscellaneous	$ -	$ (18.00)	$ 18.00
		$ -	$ -	$ -
		$ -	$ -	$ -
		$ -	$ -	$ -
	STS Expenses	$ -	$ -	$ -
Debt		$ -	$ (147.00)	
Due Date	Debt Expenses	Actual Amount	Budgeted Amount	Remainder
	Student Loan	$ -	$ (127.00)	$ (127.00)
	Credit Card	$ -	$ (20.00)	$ (20.00)
		$ -	$ -	$ -
		$ -	$ -	$ -
Savings		$ -	$ -	
Dates	Saving Categories	Actual Amount	Budgeted Amount	Remainder
	Short Term Savings	$ -	$ -	$ -
	Long Term Savings	$ -	$ -	$ -
	Future Savings	$ -	$ -	$ -
Cash Flow		$ -	$ (2.00)	

Image captured from Microsoft Excel.

Before we move onto Mike and Sarah's budget, I would like to talk to those of you with a **fluctuating, monthly income** (like Melissa). Many individuals with fluctuating income would often tell me that he or she couldn't budget because of a varying income. While I know it may feel a little less sturdy than expected income, you actually have the most opportunity, and you can budget successfully! All you need to do is determine your *salary*. Your salary is what you need to pay yourself (or make) in order to cover your expenses. In Melissa's case, her expenses each month were $1,202 (plus the extra we uncovered); therefore, she needed to make at least that—*at least* because she also had the goals of paying down debt. In order to do that rapidly, she would need to bring in more than $1,202.

So in the first month, we set a goal for her to make $2,000, and she did. Then the next month, she had to make $2,400, and she did, and so on. By setting these milestones and having goals each month, Melissa was able to steadily increase her income at a rapid pace and reach her goals successfully! Take advantage of the opportunity that you have to increase your income and meet your goals, just like Melissa did.

For those of you with a steady paycheck, that is a blessing as well. You will need to really focus on cutting your expenses like Mike and Sarah.

Mike and Sarah

If, like Mike and Sarah, you are in a positive cash-flow situation, then you are in a better spot than most.

Remember that when you first create your budget, it's just numbers on a page. Mike and Sarah actually felt like they had no money at the end of the month and felt like they were scraping by, despite what their budget had to say. On paper their cash flow looked good!

	A	B	C	D	E
1	**Budget - Mike and Sarah**				
2	©2012-2015 MAP Financial Solutions				
3					
4	**Income Categories**		$ -	$ 4,800.00	
5	Date	Income	Actual Amount	Budgeted Amount	Remainder
6		Income #1	$ -	$ 2,800.00	$ (2,800.00)
7		Income #2	$ -	$ 2,000.00	$ (2,000.00)
8		Other	$ -	$ -	$ -
15		STS Reimbursement	$ -	$ -	$ -
16					
17	**Expense Categories**		$ -	$ (3,993.00)	
18	Due Date	Personal Expenses	Actual Amount	Budgeted Amount	Remainder
19		Charity	$ -	$ (510.00)	$ 510.00
20		Rent	$ -	$ (1,495.00)	$ 1,495.00
21		Utilities - Water & Electric	$ -	$ (190.00)	$ 190.00
22		Internet	$ -	$ (40.00)	$ 40.00
23		Personal Care	$ -	$ (150.00)	$ 150.00
24		Cell Phone	$ -	$ (170.00)	$ 170.00
25		Life Insurance	$ -	$ (43.00)	$ 43.00
26		Auto Insurance	$ -	$ (90.00)	$ 90.00
27		Entertainment	$ -	$ (100.00)	$ 100.00
28		Eating Out	$ -	$ (200.00)	$ 200.00
29		Gasoline	$ -	$ (325.00)	$ 325.00
30		Groceries	$ -	$ (600.00)	$ 600.00
31		Miscellaneous	$ -	$ (80.00)	$ 80.00
32			$ -	$ -	$ -
33			$ -	$ -	$ -
34			$ -	$ -	$ -
35			$ -	$ -	$ -
49		STS Expenses	$ -	$ -	$ -
50					
51	**Debt**		$ -	$ (170.00)	
52	Due Date	Debt Expenses	Actual Amount	Budgeted Amount	Remainder
53		Student Loan	$ -	$ (170.00)	$ (170.00)
54			$ -	$ -	$ -
55			$ -	$ -	$ -
56			$ -	$ -	$ -
68					
69	**Savings**		$ -	$ -	
70	Dates	Saving Categories	Actual Amount	Budgeted Amount	Remainder
71		Short Term Savings	$ -	$ -	$ -
72		Long Term Savings	$ -	$ -	$ -
73		Future Savings	$ -	$ -	$ -
77					
78					
79	**Cash Flow**		$ -	$ 637.00	

Image captured from Microsoft Excel.

When you complete your budget and find that you have an abundance of cash flow at the end of the month, yet feel like you have none, it's safe to deduce that you are spending that money somewhere. This is why tracking your expenses is critical. As I worked with Mike and Sarah further, we were able to uncover that this money was *leaking out* and we were able to stop this by utilizing the budget. In turn they started to tell the money where to go versus wondering where it went.

While they had a positive cash flow, we still needed to address areas they could adjust. There were expenses that I felt they were overpaying on. While they did have an abundance of cash flow, they needed to save money where they could. Their cell phone bill was way too high, and while their rent was in line with their income at around 30 percent, it was on the edge of being a little too high. Reviewing expenses on a quarterly or biannual basis is a *best practice* exercise that can save hundreds if not thousands per year.

Saving money and cutting expenses reminds me of my grandfather. He taught Stephen and me a lot when we worked for him. One of the most valuable lessons he taught us was thriftiness. My grandfather was well to do, but he was always on the hunt for the best deal. His housekeeper would often tease him for cutting shampoo bottles in half in order to get the last drop of shampoo! I am not saying that you have to take it to this extreme, but some of the wealthiest people I have ever known are some of the thriftiest. Therefore, make an effort to review your expenses regularly to ensure that you're not missing out on an opportunity that is right before you!

End Destructive Patterns

Destructive patterns are habits in your life that keep you from realizing your goals. They continually pull you down. If your goal is to be financially free, which may mean being debt-free with ample savings, you have to be fully aware of the habits preventing you from getting there.

In the case of Mike and Sarah, on paper their cash-flow situation was amazing. When I first met them, they painted a picture of really struggling and having no money at the end of each month. After we sat down and reviewed their budget, I was blown away by the opportunity that I saw for them sitting on that bottom line! Their goals could be met quickly by sticking to their budget.

When we first reviewed their budget, Sarah expressed her frustration in lacking the ability to get things she needed for the kids or a house decoration here and there. And Mike was frustrated because he felt like he could not take friends to lunch or buy some of the bigger toys he had been longing for.

The issue was not a lack of cash flow, but instead a lack of tracking. While they were not putting anything on a credit card, they were spending all of their opportunity. It was time that they told their money where to go and not let it dictate to them any longer.

Let's go back to Melissa for a moment. She was using her credit card to make up for her deficit. Her credit card was offering her the lifestyle she desired. This is a destructive cycle, especially when you can't pay off the balance each month. If you only pay the minimums, the interest sucks the life out of you. It is a terrible trap; don't fall into it.

Melissa's solution to her overspending was to reduce her living expenses and increase her income. By increasing her income and sticking to her budget, she was able to pay down over $9,000 of her student-loan and credit-card debt, create a small emergency savings account, and take a trip to New Zealand!

As for Mike and Lisa, they were able to pay down all of their debt, create a nice-sized emergency savings fund, and live comfortably. They were also able to get some things they had wanted for a long time without guilt or arguing. Getting on a budget and managing it properly created less stress for each of these individuals. Circumstances don't have to dictate your success when it comes to finances—good habits do.

Finding the patterns that destroy your financial freedom comes first. Then, by changing them around, you will find the freedom you're seeking.

Part III: Tracking Spending

So this all sounds good, right? How do you make it a reality? Unfortunately putting numbers down on paper and making them perfect does not solve anything. A one-time record of your finances won't help you reach your goals.

Instead, make your budget work for you. To get the most out of it, track your expenses *weekly* against your spending, just as we discussed earlier. It's simple.

Say your gas budget is $200 per month. Every time you fill up, deduct what you spent from the budgeted amount so you know what you have left to spend for the month. This is your weekly accountability process.

Continue to use your Budget and Tracking Sheet in conjunction with each other. If you are married, you and your spouse need to be on the same page as far as your budget. One of you needs to be the Tracker. If you are single, then you're it. The Tracker is responsible for logging all spending against the budget to ensure you're staying on track. That means every week, you need to update your *Actual* and *Remainder* columns to ensure you are not overspending. If you're married, it's also the Tracker's responsibility to get a copy of the budget to the other spouse. That way your spouse always has an up-to-date understanding of where the budget stands.

Note: the Tracker is *not* the permission giver, nor the source of all budget information. It is still the Nontracker's responsibility to be in touch with the budget every week. Everyone is responsible for the spending. Stay away from the blame game.

For those of you doing the budget by hand, be sure to keep the budget notebook in a place that either of you can go to reference it at any time. For those using the MAP Budget Tool, I recommend utilizing a file-sharing service that both you and your spouse can access remotely. Stephen and I do this, and it keeps both of us on the same page at all times. We both have the mobile app on our cell phones and can access the budget at any time. By sharing a copy of the budget, you have it to reference if you are apart and you're trying to make wise financial choices.

Moving Ahead

Congratulations! You now have financial goals and a budget, two of the most important tools to reach financial freedom. Now you can put these tools to work in conjunction with your debt and savings goals to really get things moving. I am confident God is behind you, and that in your faithfulness, you will see His glory shine through in this process! Keep going and don't stop!

Chapter 10: Tackling Debt

Your budget is a tool to help you accomplish your goals, but it doesn't stop there. Not only do you have to utilize your budget on a weekly basis, you also have to implement strategy to knock out your debt and pump up your savings. This chapter will help you to strategize how to pay down your debt. It will also give you direction on what debt to pay first and how much. There is nothing more exciting than seeing the finish line in regard to your debt and, even better, crossing that finish line.

I want everyone to have access to this information and the ability to implement it with a piece of paper and pencil, so the process explained is manual. For those of you who have the ability to access a computer with Microsoft Excel, I have included a tool to help you reduce your debt. Go to www.TheStewardshipMovement.com. It does the math for you. For those of you doing the paper-and-pencil method, it won't be as sophisticated but will still bring your finances to life, which is the first step to making a change.

The most important thing I want you to remember in this process is that any debt feels like a lot. I have worked with clients who had $20,000 in debt and others with $150,000 (not including their mortgage). Debt of any size feels like a lot—because it is. It is bondage. Let's talk about why that is, and then I'll give you some tools to get your debt paid off sooner than later!

Tackling Debt

Debt is an ugly word with the capacity to conjure up ill feelings. For most of us, our financial goals entail getting out of debt and saving more. But what happens when we have to go into debt because of unforeseen circumstances? When debt is necessary in order for us to take a step in life, such as getting more education, then what?

While debt does not contribute to a healthy financial state, sometimes it is necessary. The occasional necessity of debt does not override the spiritual implications of it. Instead of making *debt free* the goal, why don't we first make handling it God's way the goal? Ultimately God wants the best for us, so His principles about debt are sure to steer us in the right direction!

When we are in debt, we are exposed, vulnerable, desperate, and trapped. Scripture has several examples of men's families and possessions being taken from them as collateral on their debt:

> Do not take a pair of millstones—not even the upper one—as security for a debt, because that would be taking a man's livelihood as security.
> Deuteronomy 24:6

> The fatherless child is snatched from the breast; the infant of the poor is seized for debt.
> Job 24:9

> Do not be a man who strikes hands in pledge or puts up security for debts; if you lack the means to pay, your very bed will be snatched from under you.
> Proverbs 22:26–27

While I don't necessarily believe that debt is a sin, it is clear that it leaves us in a vulnerable state. When we owe other people money, we can't feel free.

> The rich rule over the poor, and the borrower is servant to the lender.
> Proverbs 22:7

When Stephen and I first got married, we had about $35,000 in debt. We had the means available and decided to pay it off. Throwing that weight off our shoulders was the best feeling in the world. We were only left with our mortgages—one on our primary residence and one on a rental property. It was a feeling of jubilee! Shortly after this debt had been paid, we received notification from family that a note Stephen had taken out for a surgery needed to start having payments made on it. We were hit with an additional $30,000 in debt. Stephen and I were devastated. He had simply placed it out of his mind and hadn't wanted to think about it. While this was a hard pill to swallow, we had to face it. The honorable thing to do was to fulfill the note as quickly as possible. We both felt strongly about this. While we didn't want to give up the extra $250 a month, we knew that we needed to pay as much as we could toward it. As our income increased, we were able to pay back $500 a month. The loan went down very slowly for the nearly three years we paid on it. Toward the end of the third year of payments, Stephen and I had the means to fully pay it off. In return for this, his family cut the loan amount due in half. We were able to fulfill the note. What a blessing! God watched over Stephen's family and us. There is nothing freer than knowing that this debt is paid off and that we have honored our commitment. And for that, by God's grace, his family blessed us with their generosity. While the spiritual implications of the debt were negative, God's grace came through in the end.

As Stephen and I journeyed through this, we worked hard to adhere to the following two biblical principles regarding the debt:

1. **Pay back all debt that you borrow.**
   The wicked borrow and do not repay, but the righteous give generously...
   Psalms 37:21

2. **Pay back your debts promptly.**
   Do not withhold good from those who deserve it, when it is in your power to act. Do not say to your neighbor, "Come back later; I'll give it tomorrow"—when you now have it with you.
   Proverbs 3:27–28

I can say that by following these principles, what looked like a devastating situation turned out blessed. I believe that this blessing was due to our faithfulness to apply these two principles. I strongly urge you to live by these principles in regard to the debt that you currently have.

A third principle is to stay out of debt when you can. While not always realistic for most of us, it is best to try to stay out of debt in an effort to stay free from the bondage it creates.

3. **Stay out of debt, when you can.**
   The rich rule over the poor, and the borrower is servant to the lender.
   Proverbs 22:7

While debt does have the power to rule over us, we must remember that the only thing that should be ruling over us should be Jesus.

Pressing Forward

So you've heard it all before, but you are still thousands of dollars in debt. What's next? In congruence with the principles we've reviewed, it's time to chip away at the walls surrounding you. It is time to start to break free in order to advance the Kingdom! This process is not going to be easy, and it will require resourcefulness on your part. Draw some inspiration from the story of the Widow's Oil in 2 Kings 4:1–7:

> The wife of a man from the company of the prophets cried out to Elisha, "Your servant my husband is dead, and you know that he revered the Lord. But now his creditor is coming to take my two boys as his slaves." Elisha replied to her, "How can I help you? Tell me, what do you have in your house?" "Your servant has nothing there at all," she said, "except a little oil." Elisha said, "Go around and ask all your neighbors for empty jars. Don't ask for just a few. Then go inside and shut the door behind you and your sons. Pour oil into all the jars, and as each is filled, put it to one side." She left him and afterward shut the door behind her and her sons. They brought the jars to her and she kept pouring. When all the jars were full, she said to her son, "Bring me another one." But he replied, "There is not a jar left." Then the oil stopped flowing. She went and told the man of God, and he said, "Go, sell the oil and pay your debts. You and your sons can live on what is left."

This story is a beautiful depiction of what God calls us to do. This woman was not only combating creditors, she was also recently widowed and a new, single mother. On top of that, the creditors were threatening to take the only family she had left as collateral for her husband's debt.

Because this widow lived under the Mosaic Law, the Law condoned that her sons could be secured for the debt of her husband. The Law also included Sabbath Years and Jubilee Years. Every Jubilee Year, all slaves were to be returned to their families (Lev. 25). Instead of riding out this guarantee, the widow actively utilized the only resource she had and packaged it to pay back the debt.

I have worked with a few clients where bankruptcy was their only hope. They were thousands of dollars in debt and extremely delinquent. Because they didn't have the means or the income to pay their debt, they were subject to bankruptcy to settle their debts. In short, they were out of time. However, the majority of the clients I worked with had the means to start chipping away their debt. With concentrated effort and discipline, they were able to pay them all off. These clients included doctors who had hundreds of thousands of dollars in debt. By implementing a budget and debt-reduction plan, they methodically reduced their debts. There were also singles who, between college loans, car loans, and credit cards, had several thousands of dollars in debt. By implementing a strategy, they too were able to reduce their debts. If you are not behind on payments, then you can do this. If you have enough income to cover your bills and loan payments, then you can do this. Take heart!

Tackling debt reminds me of a lesson I learned early on in my running career. I have always admired the fast runners in races. They make it look so easy. When I first started, I never thought I could be that fast. Then, over the years and building up my fitness, I have been able to run as fast as some of the runners I admired in the past. While

I am faster, it is not any easier.

Paying down debt is much the same. Paying it down and living in a financially responsible way is not any easier for a doctor than a teacher. I have seen people who make plenty of money live beyond their means. Each of us is responsible to manage the money he or she earns. We are in charge of it; it is not in charge of us. Income is not the ultimate factor of success. While it can greatly help increase the rate at which you pay off debt, you can strategically reduce your debt with what you have *now*.

It's time to put together a plan to get your debt in order. We will explore several different ways you can strategically pay down your debt.

Note: if for any reason you are delinquent in your debt and have collectors calling, then I recommend you stop and not continue on to the next section.

Instead, seek professional help from a credit counselor ASAP. A credit counselor can sit down with you and help you analyze your debts to determine if they can work with your creditors to negotiate on your debt. I caution you to investigate the credit counselor that you decide to work with. You want to make sure you are working with a reputable firm that is interested in helping you more than itself.

Here is a checklist for you as you are seeking out credit counselors.

1. Make sure he or she is a non-profit credit counselor.

2. Set up a free consultation. This will allow you to meet with the counselor to see what his or her guidance is and to determine if it's a good fit.

3. Don't rush into bankruptcy. When hope is grim, this may seem like the best solution, but the consequences are grave. It can affect your chances to get work, loans, and housing in the future.

Above all, pray for guidance.

Tackle Your Debt

There is nothing fancy about paying off debt. With a pile of cash, we could all figure out how to pay off our debt. The main barrier for people paying off debt is their wants. For most of us, our wants are what got us into debt in the first place. Wants are all of the things outside of necessities. Debt holds us hostage; so the sooner we get out of it, the better.

In the past I was under the impression that a mortgage did not count as true debt, but the more I study the subject, the less I think this is true. Regardless of what the debt is for, it is always bondage. Therefore, as you pay off debt, be prayerful about how God is leading you to pay it off. I cannot know the timing of events that He has for you. This process is personal to each of us. So while I can't hand you the universal blue print on debt repayment, I can encourage you to knock out all debt excluding your mortgage for now—that means credit cards, car loans, student loans, personal loans, medical expenses, and beyond. Leave your mortgage loans for last, primarily because these loans tend to be the largest. And in most cases, you are dealing with an appreciating asset. A majority of your monthly payment is being paid to the bank as interest, with a small portion going toward the loan's balance (the principal). Next time you are paying your bills, take a look at your mortgage statement for this breakdown. Here's an example:

Monthly Payment	**$770.80**
Monthly Principal	$174.25
Monthly Interest	$550.63
Monthly Escrow	$45.92

You can see from this example that a majority of the payment is going toward interest. The bank is making over $6,000 each year on this loan! Only a little over $2,000 per year is going toward paying down the balance (principal). The escrow is held for homeowners insurance and property taxes.

For the future, keep in mind that you can pay more toward your principal at any time. The picture I am trying to illustrate for you here is that it can be expensive to borrow other people's money, and may cost you more in the long run (sometimes the opposite can be true).

Debt-Reduction Strategies

We are now going to discuss two strategies to pay down your debt. The first is *high interest* and the second is *low balance*. It would be my recommendation to use the snowball method with each of these to pay off your debt faster.

Strategy #1—High Interest

This strategy prioritizes paying the highest interest debts first. This strategy does not take loan balances into consideration. As you saw in the mortgage example, high interest can stifle how fast you pay off debt.

Strategy #2—Low Balance

This strategy prioritizes paying the lowest balance first. This strategy does not take interest rates into consideration. Most of the time, I recommend this strategy. It is the most rewarding because you conquer debts one by one and usually faster.

Whether you choose the high interest strategy or low balance strategy, I recommend that you utilize the snowball method to accelerate the process.

To begin, go back to your budget. How much can you allocate toward paying down your debt? (This may be dependent upon how much you want to save as well.)

Let's refer back to Tom and Lisa's budget. Their debt minimum payments total up to $504 per month. Let's say they decide to allocate $46 from their monthly cash flow toward their debt. That would make their debt-reduction budget $550 per month. As they start to pay off debt, their snowball will grow by keeping their debt-reduction budget at $550. They will continue to allocate $550 toward their debt each month, regardless of what they pay off. This method can be applied to either of the strategies we've discussed.

Create a Debt-Reduction Plan

Now for the fun part—we get to see all the numbers on one page and strategically plan how we're going to eliminate the debt! Again, we will approach this using the two methods above. If you would prefer a more automated approach, you can utilize the debt-reduction tool found on www.TheStewardshipMovement.com.

In this section you will find the manual instructions for creating a debt-reduction plan; they can also be used in conjunction with setting up your plan in the debt-reduction tool as well.

Step One—Write Down Your Debt

In order to do this step, you need to have detailed information on all of your debts: the company that you owe, the interest rate you are paying, your most recent balance, and your minimum payment amount.

Do not take this step lightly. Make sure all the information is accurate and complete so you can have a real picture of your debt.

Flip to a new page in your notebook. On the top of the page, write the header *Debt-Reduction Plan*. Then, write down the information for your debts in the format shown below. For this example, we will review Tom and Lisa's debt.

DEBT-REDUCTION PLAN

Creditor	Balance	Interest Rate	Min. Payment
Car Loan #1	$4000	7%	$225
Credit Card	$541.24	8.95%	$20
Student Loan	$7857.64	5%	$79
Car Loan #2	$7652.49	6%	$180

Step Two—Solidify Your Debt-Reduction Budget

Now determine your debt-reduction budget. In the example above, the total minimum debt payments add up to $504. Since the debt-reduction budget is $550, there is an additional $46 that can be allocated toward the debts.

Step Three—Select Your Strategy

A majority of the time, I would recommend the *low balance* strategy to clients. It is the most rewarding and exciting, and when we're talking about debt, we need this!

I would encourage you to look at your debt and the interest rates, and then think through which plan will help you reach your goals fastest. And, as always, pray for guidance and, if married, talk this over with your spouse.

Step Four—Prioritize Your Debts

Once you have settled on your strategy, reorganize the order of your debts in your notebook. In the example, I am going to recommend that Tom and Lisa utilize the low balance strategy. Therefore, we will reorganize their debts from priority one, down to priority four as shown. Then, add the extra amount to the first debt ($20+$46).

DEBT-REDUCTION PLAN

Creditor	Balance	Interest Rate	Min. Payment
Credit Card	$541.24	8.95%	$66
Car Loan #1	$4000	7%	$225
Car Loan #2	$7652.49	6%	$180
Student Loan	$7857.64	5%	$79

We have reorganized the order in which these debts appear because we want to knock out the lowest balance first; therefore, the credit card becomes the first debt we're going to eliminate.

Step Five—Update Your Budget

Once you have calculated how much you will be paying toward your debts each month, be sure to update your budget with these numbers. Tom and Lisa would need to update their budget to reflect $66 each month for the credit card versus $20. Keep track of your debt-reduction totals on this sheet as you move along.

Step Six—Celebrate

Remember to celebrate as you pay off debts! This is a *huge* accomplishment and takes dedication and focus.

What about My Mortgage?

Here are some questions to help you determine if it is time for you to tackle paying off your mortgage or not:

1. Are all of your other debts paid in full?

2. Do you have at least six months to one year's worth of income saved in liquid form (in an account that you can access with out any penalties or fees)?

3. Are you regularly contributing to a pool of money for the future that you don't and won't access until your later years?

If you can answer yes to these three questions, you may be in a position to start paying more aggressively on your mortgage. While your primary residence is not a liquid asset, your home is accumulating equity as you pay it down if its value stays above the mortgage balance. This equity is accessible (if built up) upon the sale of your home (or beforehand). A mortgage payment is also one of the largest expenses for most households each month; therefore, if you can eliminate this expense, you will have additional money that you can save toward the future or invest toward something that will increase your monthly cash flow. **My number-one caution for you is that you don't consume all of your surplus.**

If you're able to pay off your mortgage and eliminate it, don't use the money you were paying down your mortgage with for just anything. Think back to the snowball method. Use most of that additional income for something else that will grow your money.

An important balance in this is enjoying your lifestyle. So while I say don't consume all of your surplus, also be sure to do nice things for yourself that you have worked hard toward. Take time to relax and enjoy the hard work you have put in!

Debt-reduction is critical, but savings is as well. In the next chapter, we will explore how you can build up your savings while reducing your debt at the same time.

Chapter 11: Creating Savings

Too many times I hear stories of people paying off loads of debt, throwing a party, and stopping there. Paying off debt is critical to your financial success, but so is saving money. The most important thing to remember is that even if all of your debt is paid off, if you have a major expense come up with no savings, you'll end up back in debt. I want you to accomplish major milestones in slashing your debt, but I also want you to build up your savings at the same time.

Let's face it—we all have needs. These include food, clothing, water, and shelter. While we are living, we will always have these needs, and they require money. There will come a time in our lives when we may no longer be able to physically work, or we may choose not to. When this time comes, our needs will still cost money. Therefore, saving not only becomes a critical component to extra padding in life, but also may become the main source of income in our later years. In Matthew 6:25-34, Jesus urges us not to worry about what we will eat, drink, or wear. I don't believe this is a commission from Jesus to think these things will appear out of thin air. This commission goes deeper and touches back on what we spoke about in the earlier chapters; we are called not to *focus* on these things. Have you ever met anyone stressed out about these things, stressed out about money? Do you think that in all that worry and stress they can be effective for God? Be obedient to Christ where you feel He has called you. Work hard and stay focused on Him.

So where do we go from here? How do we avoid the conflict of hoarding at the expense of giving? Let's take a step back into biblical history and see how others handled savings.

Hoarding versus Provision

During the time period in which the Bible was written, wealth existed in the form of silver, gold, crops, livestock, spices, wine, and oil. These commodities were either hoarded or utilized to bless others. Many kings amassed their wealth in storehouses or store cities:

> Hezekiah received the messengers and showed them all that was in his storehouses—the silver, the gold, the spices and the fine oil—his armory and everything found among his treasures. There was nothing in his palace or in all his kingdom that Hezekiah did not show them.
> 2 Kings 20:13

> Hezekiah had very great riches and honor, and he made treasuries for his silver and gold and for his precious stones, spices, shields and all kinds of valuables. He also made buildings to store the harvest of grain, new wine and oil; and he made stalls for various kinds of cattle, and pens for the flocks. He built villages and acquired great numbers of flocks and herds, for God had given him very great riches.
> 2 Chronicles 32:27-29

> Jehoshaphat became more and more powerful; he built forts and store cities in Judah and had large supplies in the towns of Judah.
> 2 Chronicles 17:12-13

> They enter Aiath; they pass through Migron; they store up supplies at Micmash.
>
> Isaiah 10:28

While some leaders may have utilized these storehouses to hoard and showcase wealth, they were also used to do great good. Within the temple of God, storerooms held offerings of grain, incense, new wine, and oil for those who served in the temple:

> At the end of every three years, bring all the tithes of that year's produce and store it in your towns, so that the Levites (who have no allotment or inheritance of their own) and the aliens, the fatherless and the widows who live in your towns may come and eat and be satisfied, and so that the Lord your God may bless you in all the work of your hands.
>
> Deuteronomy 14:28-29

> Hezekiah gave orders to prepare storerooms in the temple of the Lord, and this was done. Then they faithfully brought in the contributions, tithes and dedicated gifts...
>
> 2 Chronicles 31:11-12

> Moreover, we will bring to the storerooms of the house of our God, to the priests, the first of our ground meal, of our grain offerings, of the fruit of all our trees and of our new wine and oil. And we will bring a tithe of our crops to the Levites, for it is the Levites who collect the tithes in the towns where we work. A priest descended from Aaron is to accompany the Levites when they receive the tithes, and the Levites are to bring a tenth of the tithes up to the

house of our God, to the storerooms of the treasury.

Nehemiah 10:37–38

In these times, accumulating wealth was done by storing away silver, gold, crops, livestock, spices, wine, oil, and armory. One could accumulate wealth simply for future provision or to hoard it.

Commenting on the argument of Christians' saving of money. Scripture shows that saving wealth (money) for future provision is wise, not ungodly. Look at what God commanded Noah to do with his family and animals:

> "You are to take every kind of food that is to be eaten and store it away as food for you and for them (*the animals*)."
> Genesis 6:21 (Emphasis added.)

Here God commands Noah to store up food as provision. There is no hoarding here, only provision.

Proverbs reminds us:

> Go to the ant, you sluggard; consider its ways and be wise! It has no commander, no overseer or ruler, yet it stores its provisions in summer and gathers its food at harvest.
> Proverbs 6:6–8

> Ants are creatures of little strength, yet they store up their food in the summer...
> Proverbs 30:25

And Scripture doesn't just recommend that we save; it commands it—

and for the right purpose: provision. Just as we're called to store up wealth for provision, we are further commanded not to consume it:

> He who loves pleasure will become poor; whoever loves wine and oil will never be rich.
> Proverbs 21:17

> In the house of the wise are stores of choice food and oil, but a foolish man devours all he has.
> Proverbs 21:20

Here Solomon is stating that if we consume all of our wealth instead of setting it aside as provision for the future, then we will be poor. In addition to storing up wealth for future provision, we are also called to provide for our loved ones:

> O Lord, by your hand save me from such men, from men of this world whose reward is in this life. You still the hunger of those you cherish; their sons have plenty, and they store up wealth for their children.
> Psalm 17:14

> A good man leaves an inheritance for his children's children…
> Proverbs 13:22

Do you see how the commission to save has just increased? We are called to save to provide not only for our own needs, but also for the needs of those in our family.

When Jesus warns against the love of money and tells the parable of the rich fool (Luke 12:13–21), he further exemplifies that saving is not wrong, but hoarding with the wrong motive in mind is. The treasures of some kings provided false security and a sense of personal worth. While King Hezekiah was a good king, I am taken back by how quickly he showcased his wealth when the messengers came to visit him. Was it to prove his worth?

Friends, we are called to have our worth in Jesus Christ, not in our stuff. That is why in Mathew 6:19–20 Jesus says to us, "Do not store up for yourselves treasures on earth, where moth and rust destroy, and where thieves break in and steal. But store up for yourselves treasures in heaven, where moth and rust do not destroy, and where thieves do not break in and steal."

As I read these words, I imagine Jesus sitting down with Hezekiah. With chairs close together and eyes locked, Jesus gently places his hand on Hezekiah's knee. "Son, please know that your worth is in me, not in your stuff. Everything that you've accumulated will all disappear someday. When that happens, what will happen to your worth? You are much more valuable than your stuff."

While it is commanded we save to provide for our futures and families, we should not save in order to validate our worth. Are we placing our worth in our bank accounts or possessions? If the answer is yes, then we need to reevaluate. In order to righteously manage our storerooms, we first must position our hearts correctly. When we understand what Scripture has to say about the accumulation of wealth and we position our hearts correctly, we can then move forward to freedom.

Create a Savings Plan

Now that we have addressed savings from a biblical perspective, we can venture into the practical.

Saving is a valuable tool that we can use to provide for current and future events. As you set up your savings plan, there will be two types: Long-Term Savings (LTS) and Short-Term Savings (STS). In addition to these two types of savings plans that we will be discussing, I strongly urge you to meet with a licensed professional to get a savings plan set up for your future years. This money becomes the income for your future needs, and it's critical. When you meet with a licensed professional, make sure it's someone whom you trust and that he or she listens to you and manages the money the way you desire. Too many clients turn a blind eye to their investments because this area can feel intimidating and overwhelming. Don't do this; know what you are invested in and why. The goal is to get a plan in place so you can be confident about the source(s) of income for your later years.

Short-Term Savings (STS)

Do you ever have a quarterly bill pop up that you forget to budget for, or a car repair that needs to be done for which you have no savings? Or perhaps a bunch of birthdays occur in one month every year that require a large chunk of your income? Whatever the surprise occasion may be, it is important that we plan for these future events so that when they arise, we have the money to cover them. STS was Stephen's plan many years ago, and it has saved us and helped so many clients. This is a portion of your income that you set aside each month to cover expenses like automobile (oil changes, repairs), household (trash bags, laundry detergent, paper towels, toilet paper), personal care (make-up, lotion, haircuts), clothing, pet care (food, vet bills), gifts (birthday, Christmas), travel, periodic bills (insurance, trash service), and more. These are all things that you will eventually need the money for. Instead of allowing these expenses to creep up on you, your STS account will help you plan for these expenses accordingly.

Long-Term Savings (LTS)
Long-Term Savings, on the other hand, is your emergency savings fund. This account covers expenses in the event of a job loss or medical emergency. This account, along with your STS account, needs to be liquid. This means that you can transfer or withdraw money from these accounts without any penalties or fees. Most use a regular savings account both for their STS and LTS accounts.

Because the LTS account is a basic concept in comparison to the STS account, we won't discuss it much further, but what we will discuss are your savings goals. Because this account is for emergency income, you will want to start building it up slowly. Here are some basic milestones that you can incorporate into your budget:

    Milestone #1—$1,000

    Milestone #2—$3,000

    Milestone #3—$5,000

    Milestone #4—$10,000

    Milestone #5—Six Months' Income

    Milestone #6—Twelve Months' Income

The savings plan I will help you create will consist of your STS and LTS accounts. Now, let's discuss how you can set up each of these.

Your Short-Term Savings Account

Your STS account should be managed via a checking or savings account with a bank. It needs to be in the form of liquid funds and an account that you can transfer to and from without penalties or fees. I recommend you use a savings account.

As noted earlier, this account is the storeroom for funds set to be allocated to cover expenses including automobile, household, personal care, clothing, pet care, gifts, travel, periodic bills, and more. This section gives you step-by-step instructions on how to get your own STS set up today. You will not believe the freedom that your STS will add to your life! You can use these instructions if you're manually tracking or using the MAP Budget Tool.

Step One—Determine the Account

Many people have multiple savings and checking accounts. If this is you, determine which account you can dedicate to your STS. If you don't have one, open a savings or checking account through your bank.

Step Two—Create Categories

Now, flip to a new page in your notebook, and at the top create the header *Short-Term Savings*. It's time to come up with your categories.

Determine your necessity categories first. For most, these include automobile, household, personal care, clothing, pet care, gifts, and periodic bills. These are all of the expenses that you will eventually *need* money for: you have to budget for them.

Once you have created your essential categories, you may have additional cash flow that you can contribute toward nonessential categories—categories like travel, home decor, improvements, and so forth. If so, create a line between these two areas as shown in the format below:

Auto
Home
Personal Care
Clothing
Gifts
Trash Service (quarterly)
Life Insurance (annually)
_____
Travel

Step Three—Determine STS Budget

In order to create your STS budget, add up your essentials and determine how much you need to set aside each month for each. For example, if your trash service is a quarterly bill, take the total, $69, and divide it by three. That means you need to set aside $23 each month for this bill. As for varying expenses—like auto, home, clothing, personal care—review your expenses for these categories over the last twelve months and average them out. So, let's pretend that when you do this, you have found that you spent $240 over the last twelve months on personal care. To determine how much you need to set aside each month, divide $240 by twelve. This equals $20 that you will need to set aside each month for this category. Now, update your STS sheet in the format as shown to determine your STS budget. For the example, we will refer back to Tom and Lisa. You will notice that the *Amount* for some of the categories is $0. That is because Tom and Lisa don't have the income at this time to support putting money into these categories; they will require an increase in income.

SHORT-TERM SAVINGS

Category	Amount (12 mo.)	Monthly Budget
Auto	$0	$0
Home	$0	$0
Personal Care	$240	$20
Clothing	$240	$20
Gifts	$600	$50
Trash Service (quarterly)	$69	$23
Life Insurance (annually)	$270	$22.50
Travel	$0	$0

The STS budget for Tom and Lisa is $135.50 per month.

When individuals first determine their STS budget, they are a little taken back. They think, "I can't afford to allocate that much to savings!" It is important to remember that this is savings for future provision. You will need the money for these items in the near future; therefore, the money must be set aside. If you don't, how can you plan to pay for them in the future—hope that the money is there when the need arises? If the money is not there when the need arises you will be required to go into debt or utilize savings.

This has been one of the hardest practices I have had to implement with our own finances. Our STS budget is $622 per month. This is a discipline, and it might hurt a little bit. This is where a lot of us start to feel the pinch, but the STS holds us accountable, preventing us from spending frivolously and then freaking out when these expenses come up and the money isn't there. Now, I say all of this in regard to your essential categories. For the additional fun categories like travel, home decorations, improvements, and so forth, these are secondary. You may not have the extra income to allocate toward these at this time. Yet over time, as you free up more cash flow, you will be able to save toward these fun categories as well!

Step Four—Add to Budget
Now that you have a budget for your STS account, be sure to add a STS line item on your budget, with the specified amount.

Tom and Lisa will need to update their budget by eliminating their personal care and life insurance and lumping those into their STS category on their budget.

Step Five—Tracking Your STS Account
Since your STS account is one account and a pool of money, you need to track this pool of money according to each category so you know how much of this pool you can access for each category. If you are utilizing the MAP Budget Tool, then this gets tracked for you after putting in your categories and some other basic data. If you are tracking this manually, then you will follow a similar process to your budget tracking. Use a pencil, as the category balances will be constantly be changing.

Below is an example of how to track your STS account. Below the listing of your categories, you will track your monthly expenses against your various categories. You will also need to add the following columns as shown. Do this now in your notebook:

SHORT-TERM SAVINGS

Current Bal.	Category	Money In	Money Out	Bal.
$0	Auto	$0	$0	$0
$0	Home	$0	$0	$0
$0	Personal Care	$20	($15.45)	$4.55

Current Bal.	Category	Money In	Money Out	Bal.
$0	Clothing	$20	$0	$20
$0	Gifts	$50	($25)	$25
$0	Trash Service (qtr)	$23	$0	$23
$0	Life Insurance (yr)	$22.50	$0	$22.50
$0	Travel	$0	$0	$0

Tracking:

8/4	Beauty	($15.45)	Personal Care
8/15	Mart Inc.	($25.00)	Gifts

There you have it—your own STS account tracking sheet! You are now well on your way to greater freedom in this area. As I mentioned earlier, this system has helped Stephen and me tremendously. I have seen it transform the financial state of many clients, as well. I pray that it is a beneficial tool for you and your family, too. Now, let's move on to your LTS account.

Your Long-Term Savings Account

Just like your STS account, your LTS account should be managed via a savings account with a bank. It needs to be in the form of liquid funds and an account that you can transfer to and from without penalties or fees.

As noted earlier, this account is your emergency savings fund. This account consists of monies that you can access in the event of a job loss or major medical emergency. It should not be used for any of the STS categories that we have discussed so far. This account can easily be set up through your bank, or you can designate one of your current savings accounts to be your LTS. Here are five easy steps to get your

LTS set up today.

Step One—Determine the Account
Determine which savings account you can dedicate to your LTS. If you don't have one, then open a savings account through your bank.

Step Two—Write Out Your Milestones
In your notebook, flip to a new page after your STS tracking sheet and at the top write the header *Long-Term Savings*. Write out your milestones in the format as shown below:

<u>LONG-TERM SAVINGS</u>

Milestone	Amount
Milestone #1	$1,000
Milestone #2	$3,000
Milestone #3	$5,000
Milestone #4	$10,000
Milestone #5	Six Months' Income
Milestone #6	Twelve Months' Income

Step Three—Determine LTS Budget
The amount you have to allocate to your LTS will be dependent upon several things. Here is a priority chart that you can utilize each month to help determine how much to put into your LTS:

Priority #1—Giving
Priority #2—Bills and STS (essential categories)
Priority #3—Debt-Reduction, LTS, and Future Savings (balance)
Priority #4—STS (nonessential categories)

Step Four—Add to Budget

By weighing these priorities and examining your budget, you should have an amount that you can allocate to your LTS. Don't be discouraged if you don't have much of anything or zero to allocate toward your LTS. This can be the hardest area to grow; that is why creating small milestones can be so helpful!

Step Five—Tracking Your LTS Account

It's important to track your progress against your LTS milestones each month. To start this process, you will need to set date goals for each milestone—the date on which you feel like you can hit that goal. So for example, if your LTS budget is $50 per month, it will take you twenty months to hit your first milestone. Write that date down next to the milestone as shown if you are tracking manually. If you are using the MAP Budget Tool, you will be able to utilize the tab provided.

LONG-TERM SAVINGS

Milestone	Amount	Goal Date
Milestone #1	$1,000	MM/YYYY
Milestone #2	$3,000	
Milestone #3	$5,000	
Milestone #4	$10,000	
Milestone #5	Six Months' Income	
Milestone #6	Twelve Months' Income	

Awesome job—you now officially have created both your STS and LTS accounts to create the majority of your savings plan! Your next step is to sit down with a licensed professional and determine how much you can allocate in your budget toward future income. The goal is to get a plan in place so that you know that you will have sufficient income in the future.

As we discussed at the beginning of this chapter, savings is a very important piece of our financial wellness. We have also learned that when we save, we are not participating in an unbiblical or ungodly process. You now have not only the biblical foundation for God's view of money, but also the practical steps to get your financial house in order. We now come to the last topic: translating all that you have learned into legacy. The conclusion is the finale of your training phase. You are now ready to stir up *The Stewardship Movement* within your community!

Conclusion

*T*he *Stewardship Movement* isn't about you. It's about your family, your church, and your community. It's about legacy.

Your legacy consists of what you do for those you shared life with—family, friends, church members, and even strangers. Your legacy is the series of footprints that your life leaves on the hearts of those you serve. It extends beyond how you're remembered. **Your legacy is eternal.**

Part of what makes up a legacy is the way we manage the resources that God entrusts us with today. The way we manage these resources not only affects our families, those we serve, and our churches, but also the Kingdom.

My goal for you is that your legacy is one that reflects brightly with regard to your financial management and even further than this, one that eternally impacts the lives of all those you lead and serve.

The Stewardship Movement is about sharing what you've learned with others so that they, too, may live out a life of **eternal impact**—a life that creates movement in the lives around them, movement in the Kingdom, movement in advancing a common mission and goal, and movement that is not hindered by *financial chaos*.

Your legacy starts now by living out all you've learned while also training up your leaders in these principles. Together, you and your leadership can live out what you've learned about biblical financial stewardship and then equip your church members to do the same, so that *growth* becomes about *impact* and not about numbers.

This movement starts with you. It's never been tried before. If your spirit moves you to join, I am confident that, united as the body of

Christ, we can create a bigger eternal legacy—one that glorifies the Father and advances the Kingdom!

Join In
The Stewardship Movement
today at:
www.TheStewardshipMovement.com

Notes

Chapter 3

1. Edward W. Goodrick and John R. Kohlenberger III, *The Strongest NIV Exhaustive Concordance* (Grand Rapids, MI: Zondervan, 1999), 892–893.

2. "Poverty," United Nations and CyberSchoolBus, *Briefing Papers,* accessed February 24, 2015, https://web.archive.org/web/20101116183705/http://www.un.org/Pubs/CyberSchoolBus/ briefing/poverty/index.htm.

3. "Life in Tegucigalpa's City Dump," The Micah Project, accessed August 19, 2014, http://www.micahcentral.org/dumplife.htm.

4. "Poverty," United Nations and CyberSchoolBus, *Briefing Papers,* accessed February 24, 2015, https://web.archive.org/web/20101116183705/http://www.un.org/Pubs/CyberSchoolBus/ briefing/poverty/index.htm.

Chapter 4

1. John Bevere, *Relentless* (Colorado Springs, CO: Waterbrook, 2012), 98–99.

2. *Merriam-Webster Online, s.v.* "wealth," accessed March 5, 2015, http://www.merriam-webster.com/dictionary/wealth.

3. *Dictonary.com, s.v.* "white lie," accessed December 15, 2014, http:/dictionary.reference.com/browse/white+lie.

4. Randy Alcorn, *The Law of Rewards* (Carol Stream, IL: Tyndale, 2003), accessed December 15, 2014, http://www.epm.org/static/uploads/downloads/book-resources/Law_of_Rewards.pdf.

5. *Merriam-Webster Online, s.v.* "humility," accessed September 16, 2014, http://www.merriam-webster.com/dictionary/humility.

6. Edward W. Goodrick and John R. Kohlenberger III, *The Strongest NIV Exhaustive Concordance* (Grand Rapids, MI: Zondervan, 1999), 1468.

Chapter 5

1. Edward W. Goodrick and John R. Kohlenberger III, *The Strongest NIV Exhaustive Concordance* (Grand Rapids, MI: Zondervan, 1999), 1566.
2. Ibid.
3. Google, s.v. "avarice definition," accessed October 9, 2014, https://www.google.com/search?rls=en&q=avarice&ei=-3VbVfG-sA4qrsAW-qYK4Dg#rls=en&q=avarice+definition.
4. Google, s.v. "abundance," accessed October 9, 2014, https://www.google.com/#q=abundance.

Chapter 6

1. Edward W. Goodrick and John R. Kohlenberger III, *The Strongest NIV Exhaustive Concordance* (Grand Rapids, MI: Zondervan, 1999), 1448.
2. Charles Pope, "On the Sad End of Solomon—A Moral Lesson for Us All," *Archdiocese of Washington* (blog), February 8, 2012, http://blog.adw.org/2012/02/on-the-sad-end-of-solomon-a-moral-lesson-for-us-all/.
3. Jerold Aust, "Profiles of Faith: Solomon—Lesson from a Wise King," *The Good News*, accessed October 14, 2014, http://www.ucg.org/christian-living/profiles-faith-solomon-lesson-wise-king.
4. Edward W. Goodrick and John R. Kohlenberger III, *The Stron-*

gest *NIV Exhaustive Concordance* (Grand Rapids, MI: Zondervan, 1999), 1530.

Chapter 7

1. Edward W. Goodrick and John R. Kohlenberger III, *The Strongest NIV Exhaustive Concordance* (Grand Rapids, MI: Zondervan, 1999), 1556.

Chapter 9

1. Eugene E. Carpenter and Wayne McCown, *Asbury Bible Commentary* (Grand Rapids, MI: Zondervan, 1992), accessed on October 20, 2014, https://www.biblegateway.com/passage/?search=James+4%3A14-16&version=NASB.

www.ingramcontent.com/pod-product-compliance
Lightning Source LLC
LaVergne TN
LVHW090116080426
835507LV00040B/909